EUCHARISTIC
MEDITATIONS

EUCHARISTIC MEDITATIONS

EXTRACTS FROM THE WRITINGS AND INSTRUCTIONS OF SAINT JOHN VIANNEY

MADE BY

ABBÉ H. CONVERT

AND TRANSLATED BY

SR. MARY BENVENUTA O.P.

SOURCE BOOKS & ANTHONY CLARKE

NIHIL OBSTAT
G.H. JOYCE, S.J.
CENSOR DEPUTATUS

IMPRIMATUR
EDM. CAN. SURMONT
VICARIUS GENERALIS

WESTMONASTERII
DIE III JULII MCMXXIII

FIRST PUBLISHED 1923
SECOND EDITION 1960
THIRD EDITION   1962
FOURTH EDITION 1964
THIS EDITION   1993

BY

SOURCE BOOKS
P.O. BOX 794
TRABUCO CANYON CA 92678

AND

ANTHONY CLARKE
16 GARDEN COURT
WHEATHAMPSTEAD HERTS.

ISBN: 0-940147-03-3 (USA)

ISBN: 0-85650-117-4 (UK)

PRINTED IN THE U.S.A

CONTENTS

5

BIOGRAPHICAL NOTE

THOSE who, as far as humanity is able, have studied God's ways with man, bear witness to the truth of St Paul's words, that his "power is made perfect in infirmity." It would seem that he could not have chosen a much weaker weapon "to confound the strong" than Jean-Baptiste Marie Vianney, born at Dardilly, a village not far from Lyons, in 1786. In his youth, no one could have predicted that he would one day be a priest so famous that his time spent in the confessional from two in the morning, or earlier, until nine at night, would not suffice for him to hear the confessions of all the penitents who flocked to him.

At one time it seemed very unlikely that he would ever realize his wish to be a priest. One obstacle after another presented itself. During the Revolution, the danger involved in such an ambition made his parents unwilling that he should cherish it. When liberty was again granted to the Church they withdrew their opposition, but his utter lack of education and his slowness in learning seemed to make any progress impossible in the studies he then began under the Abbé Balley, Curé of Écully. He made a vow to go on foot, begging his way, to the tomb of St John Francis Regis, to ask his intercession in the matter. His prayer was answered, and he now went forward at a pace that astonished M. Balley. In 1809 he was drawn for the conscription, but on the day his column was to leave he was praying in a church, forgot the time, and came late to present himself at the office. He was sent on to join his corps alone, but met a mysterious stranger who bade him follow him, and, having led him all day by unfrequented paths, left him to the hospitality of a man and wife in a lonely house. He then disappeared, and Jean-Marie never saw or heard of him again. For some time he was in hiding at Nöes, where he won the hearts of everyone, but in the conscription of 1810 his younger brother offered to take his place, and was accepted.

On resuming his training, his lack of education, interrupted studies, and consequent backwardness, threatened to prove serious obstacles to Jean-Marie's vocation. The Vicar-General, however, hearing of his holiness and deep spiritual wisdom, said, "Very well, I will receive him : divine grace will do the rest." He was ordained priest in 1815, and was M. Balley's curate till the latter's death two years later, when Jean-Marie was appointed Curé of Ars, a little village in the department of Trevoux.

His biographer, M. Monnin, says that there was nothing outwardly attractive about him at this time. He was short, awkward, and shy; and of his language, it has been said that "he was provincial to vulgarity; his pronunciation was akin to that of the peasant class from which he sprang," and that he was a frequent offender "against grammar and syntax, not to speak of literary taste, of which he did not so much as possess the rudiments:"[1] yet his holiness and his incessant labours, prayers, and penances, effected a complete reformation at Ars. Bad language, drunkness, and quarrelling ceased. Men and women were praying in the chuch at two or three o'clock in the morning, and again at night after a hard day's work, while on Sundays there was scarcely room for the numbers who attended Mass, returned for the catechizing, went to Vespers, Compline, and Rosary, and also to hear the Curé's homily in the evening.

The fulfilment of our Lord's promise concerning the *signs* that should *follow them that believe*, and which have never been wanting to his Church in any age, is so familiar to Catholics, that they can hardly realize, perhaps, the scepticism with which modern miracles are regarded even by good and Christian people outside the Church. They cling blindly to the hypothesis that the age of miracles is past, and refuse to open their eyes to facts which investigation would prove to them to be perfectly indubitable. The

[1] *Life of Marie-Eustelle Harpain.*

examination of a process for beatification or canonization would reveal much to them if they had patience to read one through.

The miracles God wrought by Jean-Marie Vianney attracted multitudes to Ars. Some of the most remarkable were connected with the *Providence*, a home for orphan and destitute girls, which he founded in 1825. He sold all he possessed, using his slender stipend and the small allowance made him by his brother to buy the house; and, later, enlarged the building with his own hands, mixing the mortar, and cutting and carrying the stones himself. Beginning with two or three orphans, the number grew rapidly. He trusted to God for everything. Catherine Lassagne, one of the superioresses, said that, as soon as he had any money, he bought necessaries for the orphanage, and "all the rest came of itself." "The following facts," says M. Monnin, writing about 1860, "are attested by eye-witnesses who are still living."

Once when there were eighty to feed at the *Providence*, Jeanne-Marie Chanay, who worked there, came to M. Vianney, to tell him she had not enough flour to make two loaves. He told her to put her leaven into what she had, and to go on baking as usual. She says :

"I know not how it happened, but as I kneaded, the dough seemed to rise under my fingers. I could not put in the water quick enough; the more I put in, the more it swelled and thickened, so that I was able to make with a handful of flour ten large loaves of from twenty to twenty-two pounds each— as much, in fact, as could have been made with a whole sack of flour." Together with Catherine Lassagne and Marie Filliat, who witnessed the miracle, she related the details to M. Monnin.

Another day, when the stock of corn had run very low, the Curé hid the relics of St John Francis Regis among the remainder, and next day the granary was full. The Mayor of Ars and many other people ran to see the miraculous wheat, and the miller, filling his sacks with it, declared it was the finest he had ever handled.

At times when the Curé was in sore need of money for the *Providence* or some improvement he was making in the church, he met mysterious strangers who gave him what he wanted; and he often found in his drawer considerable sums of money for which he could not account.

He had a special devotion to St Philomena, his "dear little saint," as he called her, and attributed miraculous cures to her intercession.

A man implored him to heal his crippled child, but was unwilling to obey the Curé by going to confession, knowing he would be exhorted to give up playing the fiddle for dances in the neighbouring villages, by which

he made his livelihood. He made his confession, however, and on going home broke
his fiddle in pieces. At the same moment
his child sprang up and ran through the
house, crying, "I am cured!"

M. Monnin gives a letter relating to the
cure of a child of eight who had been unable
to walk :

St Romain,
March 12, 1857.

Monsieur le Missionaire,

In accordance with the desire which
you expressed at my departure, I write to
give you an account of my little boy, and
to assure you that he is perfectly cured. He
has had no return of pain. He walks and
runs as if nothing had ever ailed him; and
yet the doctors had all given him up. I am
very happy. Accept for all your goodness the sincere thanks of your very humble and respectful servant,

F. Devoulet.

At the time of the cure the child's mother
had shown an overwhelming gratitude so
displeasing to the Curé's humility that he
said, with real annoyance : "St Philomena
really ought to have cured this little thing at
home."

Far more glorious was the Curé's grace of
healing souls. He effected miraculous and
lasting conversions of long hardened sinners.

Once, when a priest asked him how he managed to combine consideration for the weakness of sinners with the exaction of a penance proportionate to the sin, he said : "I give them a light penance, and do the rest myself."

Many of his penitents have borne witness that he read in their hearts what he could not have known naturally.

Towards the end of his life he used to sigh for the time when he had had the physical strength to live on the most frugal of meals taken once in two or three days. "In those days," he said, "I got everything I wanted from the good God."

On finding that he could gain no interior power over the holy Curé, the devil attacked him externally.   Extraordinary noises and furious voices calling the Curé's name were heard at night in the presbytery; the blessed Virgin's picture and a statue of St Philomena were frequently covered with dirt, and the Curé was dragged round the room in his bed.   The bed was also set on fire one night, and the flames spread to other objects, but were stopped short, as if by a geometrically shaped barrier, at the casket holding a relic of St Philomena.

The neighbouring clergy made fun of the rumoured disturbances, and treated M. Vianney as suffering from mental derangement caused by his excessive fasting and austeri-

ties. One night, however, when he was staying at St Trivier, where he was to help in
giving the exercises of the jubilee, such a
tremendous commotion disturbed the presbytery at midnight that the other clergy
ran to tell him the house was falling. He
smilingly reassured them, and the noise
ceased. An hour later he was summoned
to hear the confession of a man who had
walked many miles to confess to him, and
he remained in the church hearing confessions till Mass. These diabolical disturbances
usually heralded some special manifestation
of divine grace to sinners, and M. Vianney
often rose after a disturbed night to find
people who had travelled all night waiting
to make their confessions to him. The Abbé
Chevalon, who witnessed the coincidence of
St Trivier, said : "I made a promise to our
Lord never again to jest about these stories
of apparitions and nightly disturbances; and
as to the Curé of Ars, I take him to be a saint."

Mysterious voices were heard and strange
occurrences also took place at the *Providence*;
but M. Vianney said when told of them : "It
is the *grappin* [1] who does it. Just laugh at
him." The *grappin* was his nickname for
this unseen enemy.

Far from being the victim of a morbid
and overwrought brain, Jean-Marie Vianney
had a sweet and tranquil gaiety of spirit,

[1] "Clutcher" or "grabber."

and was by no means lacking in a sense of humour. He treated foolish questions with gentle sarcasm. "Father," said one lady, "is my husband in purgatory?" "I have never been there," was the answer. And again : "Father, I wish you would tell me what my vocation is." "Your vocation, my child, is to go to heaven." He said to one talkative young woman, from whom he had many times heard the same story : "My child, in which month of the year do you speak least? It must be the month of February, because it has three days less in it than any other."

The blessed Curé of Ars died the death of a saint as he had lived the life of a saint. Some account of his death is given at the end of the Tenth Meditation in this book, so it is unnecessary to speak of it here.

These few facts concerning the life of Jean-Baptiste Marie Vianney, whose beatification[1] was decreed by Pius X in 1905, are taken from the *Life of the Blessed Curé d'Ars,*[2] an English translation of the biography of M. Monnin, his friend and fellow priest.

TRANSLATOR.

[1] He was canonized by Pius XI in 1925.
[2] Published by Burns & Oates

PREFACE

B EFORE crossing the threshold of the Chamber of the Last Supper, Bossuet wrote in his *Meditations on the Gospel* : "Here let us open our hearts rather than our eyes." One might, we think, repeat these words concerning this little book, and inscribe them without hesitation at the head of the first page.

If it be true that the mystery of the Eucharist becomes clearer in our thoughts by striking analogies with the feelings of man's heart, what will its resplendence be when set forth to us by the heart of a saint? And this heart being that of the Curé of Ars, so pure, so intuitive, so loving, how can ours, however cold it be, fail to be rekindled by contact with such a flame?

Such has been the thought of the author of the present volume. In a better position than anyone else to know the teaching of St Jean-Marie on the Eucharist, at the source of the most authentic information, at the centre of all memories, he has collected in biographies, sermons, local traditions, and unpublished documents, all his doctrine on the great Sacrament—a rich treasure, which is increased by sacred and touching details concerning the faith of this servant of God— his love, and his sacerdotal attitude towards the Master invisible, but really present here on earth.

We are quite sure that the *Eucharistic Meditations of the Blessed Curé of Ars* will be the delight of a multitude of souls. They will very soon discern throughout these pages "that voice of the heart" of which a poet speaks, "which alone reaches the heart."

It has been truly said (and the demonstration of it will be clearly seen in the course of these readings) that the Curé of Ars had a passion for the Eucharist. The intensity of such a love is revealed in these astonishing words : "In times of discouragement, when, after the consecration, I hold in my hands the most holy Body of our Lord, seeing myself to be only worthy of hell, I say to myself : Ah, if only I could take him with me! Hell would be sweet near him : it would not be painful to stay there suffering for all eternity if we were there together..... But then there would not be any more hell : the flames of love would extinguish those of justice."

Does not this read like one of St Teresa's finest pages ?

Some people will consider, perhaps, that the greater part of these teachings treats of what is already known, and that there is nothing perceptibly new here. It might be answered that nothing is more easily forgotten than what we think we know, and that there are times when the familiar Gospel becomes a novelty again. But in composing these *Meditations* from the substance of the instructions, sermons, and homilies of his glorious predecessor, Canon Convert has rightly thought that traditional teaching acquires in the mouth of a saint a more luminous evidence and an undeniable fruitfulness.

Although they reach us cold and colourless, without the expression of face, the ardour of voice, the gestures which animated them, the tears, beautiful to see, which made their effect irresistible, the words of the Curé of Ars have still, in this little book, an intimate demonstrative virtue and a convincing force. No power conquers like love; and we cannot repeat too often that the text of this book is a sort of light veil, the sacrament of a measureless love for Christ which sprang forth in words, by turns incorrect and sublime, from the heart of the holiest priest of modern times. Catherine Lassagne, worthy pupil of such a master, has written in her *Mémoire* : "In his instructions, he often reverted to our happiness in having Jesus Christ present in the Holy Eucharist : he spoke of it with so much unction and joy that he was often too deeply moved to finish his words—his tears made up for them."

Moreover, in following St Jean-Marie to the Chamber of the Last Supper, we may open "the eyes"—that is, of the understanding—as well as "the heart". Theologians will admire the clearness of his doctrine and the profoundness of such thoughts as seem like a translation from St Thomas Aquinas. It is by no means the first time that these facts have appeared self-evident. The words of the Curé of Ars often showed that purity of heart fathoms and formulates the Truth as easily as the effort of genius. The humble catechist had long before expressed thoughts on the Eucharistic Mystery, which we find today eloquently developed and presented as noteworthy arguments by eminent apologists. He used to say, for example : "What man could not have imagined, God has done. What man could not utter, nor conceive, and what he could never have desired—that, God in his love has uttered, conceived, and executed. Should we ever have dared to suggest to God that he should make his Son die for us, that he should give us his Flesh to eat and his Blood to drink? If all that were not true, then man would have been able to imagine things that God could not do. He would have gone further than God in the inventions of love... That is impossible."

Priests particularly will appreciate the riches of these pages and the fitness of their publication. Let us add that the remarks

and reflections serving to connect the para-
graphs drawn from the works of M. Vianney,
which are due to the pen of his devout
successor, are hardly distinguishable from
the authentic text, and blend admirably with
it; so much does contact with the saint
influence the heart and spirit of those who
cherish his memory; so much does the
meditation of his doctrine and knowledge of
his native tongue, as well as facilities for
gaining information, allow the disciples to
identify themselves with the master.

One simple but altogether astonishing fact
meets the observer's eye when he considers
the mass of modern Christians. That fact is,
that he whom the scriptural documents, the
infallible authority of the Church, Catholic
tradition, and the intuitions of the mind and
heart reveal to them as really present in the
Eucharist, is the same who will judge us at
the end of this rapid passage of time, and
from whom we expect eternal life. Yet, even
among believers, men accord him only a very
secondary attention, and give him only a very
limited worship. To what, then, must such
inconsistency be attributed?

Humble and attentive reading of these
Eucharistic Meditations will help to destroy
this indifference. All those who come to
study the great mystery at the school of the
Curé of Ars will say, like the two disciples of
Emmaus, whose *eyes were held*, when they

were so close to the Saviour : *Was not our heart burning within us, whilst he spoke in the way, and opened to us the Scriptures?* And like them, they will know their Master in the breaking of bread.

J. L. MONESTES,
Canon of Agen Cathedral

ARS,
April 27, 1905.

EUCHARISTIC
MEDITATIONS

FIRST MEDITATION

CHRIST PRESENT IN THE EUCHARIST

" A T the moment when the mother of St Alexis recognized her son in the lifeless body of the beggar who had lived for thirty years under her palace stairway, she cried out : 'O my son! that I should have known thee so late!...' The soul, at the end of this life, will see at last him whom it possessed in the Eucharist; and, at sight of the consolations, the beauties, the riches that it has disregarded, it, too, will cry out : 'O Jesus, my Life, my Treasure, my Love, to think that I should have known thee so late!...' "

Divine Saviour, while I meditate on the proofs of thy Presence under the Eucharistic veils, enlighten my mind, enkindle my heart, and inspire me with that keen and living faith which is already a vision of thine eternal beauty.

Jesus Christ is present in the Eucharist with his body, his Blood, his Soul, and his Divinity. Do you want clear and convincing proofs of it?

I. IT IS THE AFFIRMATION OF OUR LORD HIMSELF

Having taken bread in the presence of his Apostles, he said to them : "This is bread; I am going to change it into my Body : this is wine; I am going to change it into my Blood. This Body is truly the Body which shall be crucified, and this Blood is the very Blood that shall be shed for the remission of sins; and each time you pronounce these same words," said he again to his Apostles, "you will work the same miracle, and you will communicate this power one to another to the end of the world."

Jesus Christ is the Truth; his Presence in the Eucharist is then a fact as certain as it is adorable. But "argument is unnecessary to Christians who have so many times tasted the sweetness communicated to them by God in the sacrament of love." O Eucharist, I believe in thee; I believe, O Jesus, that "thou art in this sacrament as truly as thou wast for nine months in Mary's womb," as really as "thou wert on the Cross."

II. IT IS A FACT OF EXPERIENCE

" 'Do you believe that a morsel of bread can detach itself all alone and go and place itself unaided on the tongue of one who draws near to receive it' I asked one day of two Protestant ministers who did not believe in the real Presence of our Lord.—'No.'—'Then it is not bread.'

"This is, indeed, the fact which I witnessed. A man had temptations to doubt the real Presence. 'What does one know about it? It is not certain. The Consecration—what is it? What happens on the altar at that moment?' But he desired to be rid of these temptations, and prayed the blessed Virgin to procure him a simple and tranquil faith. Now listen to me. I do not say that it happened *somewhere*; I say that it happened to *me*. Directly that man came to receive Communion the sacred Host detached itself from my fingers, when I was still at a good distance, and went of itself to rest on that man's tongue."[1]

III. IT IS A FACT IN ACCORDANCE WITH REASON

"Our Lord said : *Whatsoever you shall ask of my Father in my name, he will give it you.* We should never have thought of asking God for his own Son. But what man could not have imagined, God has done. What man could not utter nor conceive, and what he could never have dared to desire—that, God in his love has uttered, conceived, and executed. Should we ever have dared suggest to God that he should make his Son die for us, that he should give us his Flesh to eat

[1] *Esprit*, 62-63.

and his Blood to drink? If all that were not
true, then man would have been able to
imagine things that God could not do. He
would have gone further than God in the
inventions of love... That is impossible."

IV. IT IS A FACT ESTABLISHED BY HISTORY

Let us cite only one example : "A priest
was saying Mass in a church of the town of
Bolsena, and, after pronouncing the words of
consecration, doubted the reality of the Body
of Jesus Christ in the Sacred Host. At the
same instant the sacred Host was all covered
with blood. It seemed as though Jesus
Christ would reproach his minister for his
infidelity, and make him sorry for it, and at
the same time show us, by this great miracle,
how firmly convinced we ought to be of his
holy Presence in the Eucharist. The sacred
Host shed blood with such abundance that
the corporal, the cloth, and the altar itself
were covered with it. The Pope, who was
informed of this miracle, ordered that this
corporal, all blood-stained, should be brought
to him; and, being sent to the town of Or-
vieto, it was received there with great pomp,
and exposed in the church. Every year this
precious relic is still carried in procession on
the feast of Corpus Christi. Ought not that
to confirm our faith? But, my God, what
need of proofs have we after the very words
of Jesus Christ?"

EXAMPLE

The Curé of Ars had received the gift of faith in eminent perfection. His union with God had, so to speak, rendered revealed truths sensible and palpable to him. What we perceive from a distance, vaguely, confusedly, through an image, in an enigma, he saw in itself with a direct and steady gaze.

"We only have a faith a thousand miles away from its object, as if the good God were on the other side on the sea," he used to say. "If we had a living, penetrating faith like the saints, we, like them, should see our Lord. *There are priests who see him every day at Mass.*"

Was it not of himself that the blessed Curé was speaking? We may think so, especially if we remember the following facts :

One day, when he seemed quite sad, the matrons of the *Providence* asked the reason of his sadness, and he replied, "I have not seen our Lord for several days..."

"You see him, then?" they said. But he changed the conversation.

Another day he was taking his meal, standing, in the parlour at the *Providence*. Believing himself alone, he said with a long sigh, "I have not seen the good God since Sunday." He was heard by Marie Chanay, who, approaching him, asked if he had seen him before. He was silent.[1]

[1] *Sommaire*

May we not infer from this that the Eucharist had no veils for him, and that our Lord showed himself openly to his servant almost habitually?

O blessed Jean-Marie, pray for us and procure us the grace of a living faith in Christ's Presence in the Eucharist.

SECOND MEDITATION

CHRIST'S LOVE IN INSTITUTING
THE EUCHARIST—I

CHRIST, "having loved his own... loved them to the uttermost." Is it not, indeed exceeding love which makes Jesus perpetuate his Presence among his disciples? He gives them an inestimable gift; he secures to them an all-powerful remedy against the world's tribulations; he opens to them a source of singular grace. Let us meditate on these marvels of the divine charity.

The love of Jesus Christ in the institution of the Eucharist is revealed:

I. BY THE GIFT HE THEREBY MAKES TO US

"By the Eucharist he feeds his children, not with ordinary food, nor with the manna by which the Jewish people were fed in the wilderness, but with his sacred Body and his precious Blood. Who could ever think of such a thing if it were not himself who says it, and, at the same time, brings it to pass? Has the tenderness of a father, or a king's generosity to his subjects, ever been known to go so far as that of Jesus Christ in the Sacrament of our altars? Parents leave their goods to their children in their wills, but in the testament of Jesus Christ, they are not temporal goods that he bequeaths to us; it is he who gives us himself with his divine riches. Is not this a veritable prodigality of a God for his creatures? Oh, how worthy are these marvels of our wonder and our love! A God, having taken our weakness upon him," makes himself the food of our souls. "O people of Christendom, how blessed are you in having so good and so rich a God!"

II. BY THE END FOR WHICH HE THEREBY OFFERS HIMSELF

"Knowing that the time has come to return to his Father, he cannot bring himself to leave us alone on the earth among so many enemies who all seek nothing but our ruin. He wants us to have the blessedness of finding him whenever we will; and by this great Sacrament he pledges himself to remain in the midst of us, day and night, to be our Father, Consoler, and Friend. Happier than those who lived during his mortal life, when he was only in one place. we find him today in every corner of the world; and this happiness is promised to us till the end of time. Oh, tremendous love of a God for his creatures! How great is the tenderness of the Father!"

III. BY THE GRACES HE GIVES US THEREIN

What does Jesus Christ do in the Eucharist? It is "a God who, as our Saviour, offers himself each day for us to his Father's justice.

If you are in difficulties and sorrows, he will comfort and relieve you. If you are sick, he will either cure you or give you strength to suffer so as to merit Heaven. If the devil, the world, and the flesh are making war upon you, he will give you weapons with which to fight, to resist, and to win the victory. If you are poor, he will enrich you with all sorts of riches for time and for eternity. Let us open the door of his sacred and adorable Heart, and be wrapped about for an instant by the flames of his love, and we shall see what a God who loves us can do. O my God, who shall be able to comprehend?"[1]

EXAMPLE

Nothing can give an idea of the blessed Curé's devotion to the Holy Eucharist. He gave it the sweetest and tenderest names; he invented new expressions by which to speak of it fittingly. It was his favourite subject, and he was perpetually returning to it in his instructions. Then his heart would dissolve in gratitude and love; his face was illumined, his eyes blazed; his soul, which was that of a saint, was pierced as by an arrow : tears choked his voice.

He called Communion *un bain d'amour*.[2]
... He often said : "In times of discourage-

[1] Sermon for Holy Thursday. Sermon for Corpus Christi.

[2] Literally "a bath of love."

ment when, after the consecration, I hold in
my hands the most holy Body of our Lord,
seeing myself to be only worthy of hell, I
say to myself : 'Ah, if only I could take him
with me!   Hell would be sweet near him :
it would not be painful to stay there suffering
for all eternity if we were there together...
But then there would not be any more hell :
the flames of love would extinguish those of
justice.' "

One Christmas night he was singing Mass,
and waited till the singing should end after
the elevation, to intone the *Pater Noster*.
Meanwhile he was gazing at the sacred Host,
which he held in his hands above the chalice;
great tears fell from his eyes, and a gentle
smile played on his lips.   "What were you
thinking of just then?" his curate, M. Tocan-
nier, asked him in the sacristy.

"*Mon camarade*, I was saying to our Lord,
'My God, if I knew that I was to be damned,
now that I hold thee, I would not let thee go
again.' "

Towards the end of his life he hardly ever
preached without speaking of this great
Sacrament. Once, when circumstances obliged
him to give the instruction in the choir of the
church, the nearness of the Blessed Sacrament
caused him such strong emotion that he was
obviously at pains to find another subject on
which to speak.[1] He delighted to speak of the

[1] *Sommaire.*

Holy Eucharist in conversation, and his words bespoke such conviction and such love for our Lord, that all who heard them were deeply moved.[1]

O blessed Jean-Marie, pray for us, and obtain for us a burning love for the God of the Eucharist.

[1] *Sommaire.*

THIRD MEDITATION

CHRIST'S LOVE IN INSTITUTING
THE EUCHARIST—II

THE consumation of love is "that a man lay down his life for his friends." It was of thyself thou wast speaking, O Jesus, in saying these words. In order to give thy life for me in the Eucharist, thou hast abandoned thy Sacrament to the profanations of the wicked, and thou comest to me only by undergoing derision and irreverences. At the moment when thine enemies are preparing thee a crown of thorns, nails, and a cross, thou art preparing for me a chalice of benediction and the Bread of Heaven. Oh, how eloquently thou speakest to me herein of the might of thy love. Grant that it may enkindle my soul in this meditation.

Three things show forth Jesus' love for us in the institution of the Eucharist :

I. THE CONTEMPT TO WHICH HE EXPOSES HIMSELF

"He knew well, before he instituted this sacrament of love, to how much contempt and profanation he was going to expose himself." O my Saviour, would that thou mightest remain in heaven after thou hadst ascended there! There, at least, "the angels

would love thee with a pure and perfect love";
but in the Eucharist the Jews pierce thee
again with nails, and bad Christians receive
thee unworthily, "some without contrition,
others without desire of amendment, others,
perhaps, with crime in their hearts." He
knows it, "but all this has no power to stop
him; it is his will that his Body, his Soul,
and his Divinity may be found in all places
of the world, and that with him we may find
every happiness." He wills to be our life at
his own expense—to be our adoration, our
thanksgiving, our prayer, and our propitia-
tion.

II. THE DAY ON WHICH HE INSTITUTED
THIS SACRAMENT

"How great was the charity of Jesus Christ
in choosing for the institution of the Eucharist
the eve of the day on which he was to be put
to death! At that moment all Jerusalem is
on fire, all the populace enraged, all are
plotting his ruin, and it is precisely at that
moment that he is preparing for them the
most unutterable pledge of his love. Men
are weaving the blackest plots against him,
and he is only occupied in giving them the
most precious gift he has. They are only
thinking of setting up an infamous cross for
him that they may put him to death, and he
is only thinking of setting up an altar that
he may immolate himself every day for us.

They are preparing to shed his Blood, and Jesus Christ wills that this same Blood shall be to us a draught of immortality for the consolation and happiness of our souls. Yes, we may say that Jesus Christ has loved us even to exhausting the riches of his love."

III. SOME CIRCUMSTANCES OF THE INSTITUTION

"He chose, for the institution of the Eucharist, *bread and wine*, the food of all men, rich and poor, the strong as well as the languishing, to show us that this heavenly food is for all Christians," small and great, vassals and kings. "Come to me, all you that suffer; no one is excluded from the feast that I prepare for you."

He consecrates the wine in a chalice. "We read in the writings of St John[1] that the Apostle saw an angel to whom the eternal Father had given the cup of his wrath to pour out upon all nations; but here we see just the contrary. The eternal Father gives into his Son's hands the cup of his mercy to be poured out upon all nations of the earth. Speaking to us of his adorable Blood, he says to us as to his Apostles : '*Drink ye all of this*, and you will find therein the remission of your sins and eternal life.' O happiness unutterable... O blessed fountain!"

"When Jesus Christ worked this great

[1] *Apocalypse* 16. 19.

miracle" of the consecration, "he raised his eyes to heaven and gave thanks to his Father, showing us how much he desired that happy moment for us. 'Yes, my children,' our divine Saviour seemed to say then, 'my blood is impatient to be shed for you, my body burns with the desire to be torn for the healing of your wounds, and the thought of my suffering and death overwhelms me with joy, because you will find therein a remedy for all your ills.' Oh, what love is there like this of a God for his creatures?[1]

EXAMPLE

The Eucharist was the centre towards which all M. Vianney's thoughts and affections converged. He spoke of it is terms naïve and full of poetry, such as love alone can find, and which, once heard, are never effaced from the memory or the heart. The Eucharist was for him the adored Master who, before all others, had a right to his homage.

"I was ten years old," wrote an ecclesiastic shortly after the death of the blessed Curé; "it was in 1820, and in the courtyard of the Collège de Meximieux, where I went to school, we were practising throwing flowers for the Corpus Christi procession, when I saw approaching a priest of very simple, poor,

[1] Sermon for Corpus Christi, 1st point. Sermon for Holy Thursday.

and humble appearance. One of my companions said to us, 'That is the Curé of Ars; he is a saint... He lives on nothing but boiled potatoes.' I regarded him with astonishment. When someone addressed a few polite words to him, he stopped a moment, and said, smiling kindly : 'When you throw flowers before the Blessed Sacrament, my boys, hide your hearts in your baskets, and send them to Jesus Christ, among the roses.'

"Then, without paying any other visit, he crossed the courtyard and turned into the college chapel to salute the Master of the house in his tabernacle. I have forgotten nearly all the names of the schoolfellows I had then, and almost all that happened under my eyes : but the name of that priest, his visit to the Blessed Sacrament, and the words of my companion, have never gone out of my mind. I was especially struck (for I was very greedy) by the thought of a man living only on potatoes. I understood, without knowing why, that here was something rare and prodigious."

O blessed Jean-Marie, pray for us and obtain for us grace to make amends, by a generous love, for the outrages that Jesus receives in the Blessed Sacrament.

FOURTH MEDITATION

EXCELLENCE OF THE SACRAMENT OF THE EUCHARIST

I WILL *praise thee, O Lord, with my whole heart, in the council of the just* (Ps. 110. 1-5). Creation and the government of the universe are great works which show thy power, thy wisdom, and thy mercy; but nowhere do they shine as in the Eucharist, memorial of the wonders that thou hast wrought on earth. I consecrate my voice, my heart, and my mind to thy praise; give me the love and reverence of the cherubim and seraphim who adore thee with holy trembling.

I. THE POWER OF GOD'S GOODNESS SHINES IN THE EUCHARIST MORE THAN IN CREATION

"If we consider all that God has made, heaven and earth, and that beautiful order which reigns in this vast universe—all manifests an infinite power which has created all things, an admirable wisdom which governs all things, and a supreme goodness which provides for all with the same facility as if it were occupied with one creature alone; and all these marvels cannot but fill us with admiration and astonishment.

"But if we speak of the adorable Sacrament of the Eucharist, we may say that here is the marvel of the love of a God for us. Here it is that his power, his grace, and his goodness shine in a manner altogether extra-ordinary. Here is the bread come down from heaven, the bread of angels, which is given us for the food of our souls; here is the bread of strengthening which comforts and sweetens our sorrows, the traveller's bread, the key which opens heaven to us. 'He that receiveth me,' said the Saviour, 'shall have eternal life.' And to give us this bread, Jesus multiplies miracles, turns the world of nature upside down, and suspends all its laws." [1]

II. HIS LIBERALITY AND MERCY ARE HERE MANIFESTED MORE VIVIDLY THAN IN THE OTHER SACRAMENTS

None "can be compared to the Eucharist. By Baptism, it is true, we receive the title of God's children; heaven is opened to us in consequence, and we are made participators in all the treasures of the Church. By Penance, the wounds of our soul are healed, and the friendship of God is restored to us. By Confirmation, Jesus Christ gives us the Spirit of light and power. By Extreme Unction, he clothes us with the merits of his death and passion. By Holy Orders, he communicates to the priest all his powers. By Matrimony, he sanctifies all our actions, even those in

[1] Sermons, ii, 127.

which man seems only to follow natural inclinations. Mercies truly worthy of a God who is in all things infinite!

"But all this seems to be only an apprenticeship of his love for men : in the adorable Sacrament of the Eucharist he goes further." [1] He gives us himself; we receive here not the application of his precious Blood, but the author of grace as well.

The Eucharist is Jesus in all his different states : it is Nazareth where he renews his Incarnation, Bethlehem where he is mystically born, Galilee where he continues to teach souls and to move them with his grace, the Calvary on which he offers himself in sacrifice. It is Jesus prolonging his life and his benefits in our midst. O inestimable grace, immense, incomprehensible, divine liberality.

EXAMPLE

"If we loved our Lord," said M. Vianney one day, "we should have that gilded tabernacle, that house of the good God, always before our mind's eye. When we see a spire from the road, that sight ought to make our hearts beat like the heart of a lover at sight of the roof under which his love dwells. We ought to be unable to take our eyes off it." [2]

In these circumstances, he did not resist the desire of entering a church, there to

[1] Sermons, 242, 376-377   [2] *Esprit*, 295.

adore him to whom he lived always so intimately united. On his way back from Dardilly after his first flight,[1] finding himself at Beaumont with M. Raymond, his curate, he passed a church. "Let us go in," he said to his companion. The two travellers knelt down to say part of the Office. When they rose they saw, to their great astonishment, that the church was full of the faithful, as if they had been summoned by the sound of the bell. M. Vianney mounted the pulpit, and gave a moving address to this multitude.

O blessed Jean-Marie, pray for us, and obtain for us grace to conceive a great esteem for this most sacred and holy of the sacraments.

[1] The blessed Curé of Ars made more than one fruitless effort to escape secretly from Ars and the crowds which his fame had attracted, that he might go away, as he said, "to weep over his poor sins."—*Translator.*

FIFTH MEDITATION

THE EUCHARIST THE FOOD OF THE SOUL

"I N every house there is a place in which the household provisions are kept : it is the store-cupboard. The Church is the house of souls. To us who are Christians it is our own house. Well, in this house there is a store-cupboard. Do you see that tabernacle? If anyone were to ask Christians, 'What is that?' they would reply : 'That is the store-cupboard.' There is the Body of Jesus, and there is his Blood; and this good Saviour said to us : *Take ye and eat... take ye and drink.*" [1]

"A mortal man, a creature, feeds himself, satiates himself, with his God, taking him for his daily bread, his drink... O miracle of miracles!... O love of loves!...
O joy of joys!" [2]

I thank thee, O my God, and ask of thee grace always to hunger after this heavenly food.

I. THE BODY AND BLOOD OF JESUS CHRIST THE FOOD OF OUR SOULS IN THE EUCHARIST

"Every created being must be fed in order to live; that is why the good God has made trees and plants grow—they are a well-

[1] *Esprit*, 141-142.   [2] Sermons, ii, 246.

furnished table to which all the beasts come
to get their own proper food.

"But the soul also must be fed. Where,
then, is its food? When God desired to
give a food to our soul to sustain it in the
pilgrimage of life, he looked upon creation
and found nothing that was worthy of it.
Then he turned again to himself, and resolved
to give himself... O my soul, how great
you are, since only God can satisfy you!
The food of the soul is the body and blood
of a God. O glorious food! The soul can
feed only on God; only God can suffice it;
only God can fill it; only God can satiate
its hunger. Its God is absolutely necessary
to it." [1]

O my soul, bless this God, who is so great!
Come often to this divine banquet to take
your fill of justice and holiness. Those who
refuse to sit at this banquet, or who partake
of it only at long intervals, condemn themselves to certain death or to wasting away;
for we cannot live without eating, nor enjoy
vigorous health without eating frequently.

II. INDIFFERENCE OF CHRISTIANS FOR THE EUCHARISTIC BREAD

"My God, how can it be that Christians
actually remain so long without giving this
food to their poor souls? They leave them
to die of want." [2]

[1] *Esprit*, 140-141. [2] Sermons, ii, 246.

"They are close to this glorious Sacrament, like a person dying of thirst by the side of a river, when he has only to bend his head... like a person remaining in poverty with a treasury close beside him, when he has only to stretch out his hand."[1] "My God, what misery and blindness... when they have so many remedies for healing their souls, and such food for preserving their health!... Alas! let us sorrowfully admit that man grudges nothing to a body which sooner or later will be destroyed and eaten by worms; while a soul created in the image of God, a soul which is immortal, is despised and treated with the utmost cruelty...

"Tell me what it can profit you to leave your soul in so unhappy a state by depriving it of the food which alone can create strength and give it vigour. You are contented and at peace, you say... Is it because your soul is only awaiting the moment when death will strike it and drag it to hell?"[2] Is it because you are vegetating in mediocrity and tepidity?

"What confusion you would feel, if your faith were not extinguished or weakened, to see a father or mother, a brother or sister, a friend or neighbour, go to the holy table to be fed with the adorable Body of Jesus Christ and yourself abstaining from it! My God, what a misfortune—so much the greater because we do not comprehend it!"[3]

[1] *Esprit*, 137.   [2] Sermons, 246.   [3] *Ibid.*, 248.

"Do not say," to justify your estrangement from the holy table, "that you have too much to do. Has not the divine Saviour said : 'Come to me all ye that labour and are exhausted: come to me, I will relieve you.'" Can you resist an invitation so full of love and tenderness? "Do not say that you are not worthy of it. It is true you are not worthy, but you have need of it. If our Lord had been thinking of our worthiness he would never have instituted his glorious sacrament of love, for no one in the world is worthy of it—not the saints, nor the angels, nor the archangels, nor the blessed Virgin... but he was thinking of our needs.

"Do not say that you are sinners, that you are too wretched, and that that is why you dare not approach it. You might just as well say that you are too ill, and that that is why you will not try any remedy nor send for the doctor."[1]

EXAMPLE

Soon after M. Vianney's installation at Nöes he went to see the curé of the parish. The latter conceived such a high idea of the young man's piety, that, rigorist though he was, he proposed to admit him to frequent Communion. The servant of God accepted this unexpected offer with unspeakable joy, and communicated almost every day.

[1] *Esprit*, 144-145.

Having become curé at a time when the custom of frequent Communion did not exist in France, St Jean-Marie was one of the first promoters of this holy practice, and he always earnestly exhorted the faithful to it, both in the pulpit and in the confessional. [1]

At Ars people received Communion at the great feasts. It was the custom among the majority of the mothers of families, and the girls, if they were not too fond of dancing; but the practice of frequent Communion, so simple and so vital, was unknown there. The zealous pastor lamented over it. "I can do no good here," he said sorrowfully, "I am afraid of being damned in this place... Oh! if I could only see our divine Saviour known and loved! If I could distribute his most sacred Body every day to a great humber of the faithful, how happy I should be!"

He was specially eloquent when he preached on the Holy Eucharist, and represented it as the true food of the soul—heavenly food, which alone can satisfy it; for, to his mind, all besides was like a pebble in the mouth of a starving man, and could not satisfy the sacred hunger of the soul. [2]

"I have done my utmost," he said, "to get my men to communicate four times a year. If they had obeyed me they would all be saints." [3]

[1] *Sommaire.*　　　　[2] *Ibid.*　　　　[3] *Ibid.*

His efforts were not in vain. At the end
of a very short time, a new seed of salvation,
and the most fruitful of all, was deposited in
that soil that had been considered stricken
with barrenness. Communions became more
numerous, especially among the women and
girls; a good number began to communicate
every fortnight, others more often; and each
year a certain number of men communicated several times. There were no country
parishes where frequent Communion was
held in more honour than at Ars; and, by
the care of St Jean-Marie, the observance
of Sundays and feast-days became a distin-
guishing feature of that little village.

O blessed Jean-Marie, pray for us, and
obtain for us an ardent desire of Holy Communion.

SIXTH MEDITATION

THE SUNDAY BANQUET

"GIVE us this day our bread."
"There are two parts of us—the soul and the body. We ask the good God to feed our poor *carcase*,[1] and he responds by making the earth produce all that is necessary for our subsistence. But we ask him also to feed our soul, which is the fairest part of ourselves; and the earth is too small to furnish what will satisfy our soul; it is hungry for God—nothing but God can fill it. So the good God has not thought it too much to dwell on earth and to take a body, in order that that body might become the maintenance of our souls. Our Lord has said : *My flesh is meat indeed... The bread that I will give is my flesh for the life of the world.*"[2]

O Jesus, give me this living bread which strengthens the soul, beautifies, enkindles, and satiates it.

I. IT IS FITTING THAT THE IMMORTAL SOUL SHOULD HAVE ONE GOOD MEAL A WEEK

"The third commandment is most important. Thou shalt keep the Sundays by devoutly serving God. The week is for things material, Sunday for the spirit.

---

[1] *Cadavre*, literally "corpse."   [2] *Esprit*, 114-115.

"The body, made of clay, rots and falls to ruin; the soul, the image of God, is imperishable, and it is this that sustains the body. It is, then, to this that we owe most care, and yet we habitually neglect the soul that we may take care of our body.

"Behold, all the week men gather, lend, buy, sell. Well and good; but all that is for the body. Arrange, then, to make a good feast once a week for your immortal soul.

"O sweet banquet, heavenly bread! Ah, what a privilege to be able to feed our souls, and to feed them on God!"

II. AND WHEN IS THIS GOOD MEAL TO BE MADE?

"On Sundays at least. O day of the good feast! I know that it is only imposed on you once a year—at Easter; but must we be forced to be happy? And when we may have a divine meal every day, shall we have such bad taste[1] as not to take it?...

"The feast of the holy table is the good God in us. The great sages of antiquity could not understand this extraordinary thing; they said that God was too great to become incarnate that he might give himself to us. It was because they did not know to what lengths the goodness of God goes.

"But *we* know it. What a knowledge!

---

[1] There is here a pun, less evident in English, the French word *goût* being more closely connected with the idea of food than the English "taste".

God has come into ourselves, and we can reach to him. Ah! if we would, we might be angels on earth.

"O beautiful life—happy life! To live on God—live on God at least on Sunday! Take care, lest without God you are lost. Have we, then, no hunger for God? Is it too much to feed upon God one day in seven?

"My body eats its fill, but my soul? If it is not hungry, it must be very ill...

"Ah! love God, live on God, serve God. That is happiness."

III. PREPARING OURSELVES FOR THIS BANQUET OF THE SOUL BY PURITY

"We must go to some trouble in taking care of our souls. Look at those images of the most blessed Virgin and St Philomena : the painter has worked hard to adorn them, and that is why they are beautiful and please the eye. Let us too work hard for the adorning of our souls, that they may give pleasure to men and angels and the good God.

"Nothing is so beautiful as a pure soul, a soul nourished by its God. Purify yourselves then by a good confession, and each Sunday give your soul a good meal.

"You know that one perceives the good odour and savour of fruit in proportion as the body is healthy : so the soul tastes and penetrates the excellence of God according to the measure of its purity.

"Ah! for want of purity we do not relish God. What unhappiness not to taste him, this good God! Let us purify ourselves, receive our God, and merit heaven. In heaven we shall see our own beauty, and taste all the sweetness of God."

IV. DESIRING HIM ARDENTLY

"Think, if one only reflected on it... that priest—he holds God for the feeding of my soul. Ah! we should die of gladness.... But we do not love the good God, not we.

"Why, the good God is so good, so great, that we must fly joyously and high as a bird to reach him. And what a song of happiness when we have attained to him! Judge then of the joy of having this great God for our very food.

"What then is the soul to deserve this? O my soul, who is it that you are going to receive? Your God, your Creator and your Saviour. Ah, my children, if we only understood, we should die of gladness."

V. EFFECTS OF THIS BANQUET ON SOUL AND BODY

"One meets with good Christians who forget their bodies; that is surely better than being like bad Christians who forget their souls, like people of the world who think only of material things. There they are, filling themselves with the most abundant and delicate food, and what is the result? When all is said and done, a corpse carried to the cemetery.

"For us Christians the fruit of our spiritual food is the salvation of our soul, Heaven, our body itself transfigured.

"Do you understand? To ascend to heaven! To be filled with God! Man is so great, so great, that he reaches as high as the shoulder of God.

"See how great is the fruitfulness of this good meal. The Holy Communion fed St Simeon's body and soul together; and his soul, flooded with the joy of loving God, sustained his body."

EXAMPLE

In the tribunal of penance, the direction of M. Vianney concerning Holy Communion was simply a confirmation of his instructions and the doctrine he proclaimed from the pulpit.

A lady from Beaujolais confessed to him one day. She had inclinations to piety, but communicated very rarely.

"Communicate once a fortnight," M. Vianney said to her.

"It is not customary where I live."

"You will make it so. Go, my child."

In another confession, he exhorted her to weekly Communion.

"But Father, I am already the only fortnightly communicant.... What will people say if they see me going to the holy table every Sunday?"

"You have many friends, my child?... Choose the most virtuous among them, and persuade them to communicate once a week like yourself; then you will not be alone. Afterwards, bring them to me."

St Jean-Marie's penitent finally determined to practise weekly Communion, kindled enthusiasm round her, and soon returned with two companions resolved to imitate her.

M. Vianney heard their confessions.

"My children, make yourselves apostles of the Holy Communion, and encourage the practice of it by your advice no less than by your example. Come back in six months, and bring me, each of you, two or three companions won over to your cause."

They put forward some difficulties, but finally promised.

Six months later these devout girls knelt again at the feet of the holy curé, triumphant this time, for their number had multiplied beyond all hopes. There were a dozen resolved to communicate every Sunday and even oftener.

The curé of the parish, astonished at a fervour of which he did not know the cause, made inquiries; and when he knew the origin of this movement which brought souls nearer to our Lord and inaugurated an era of holiness among the faithful confided to his care, he hastened to go himself to thank M. Vianney.

O blessed Jean-Marie, pray for us, and obtain us the grace to make a good Communion every Sunday.

SEVENTH MEDITATION

THE EUCHARIST UNITES US
TO JESUS CHRIST

HE *that eateth me, the same also shall live by me.* It is thou, O my God, who wilt be his life. What a transformation life works where it meets no obstacle. From lifeless dust, from a little clay, it brings forth a flower which delights us by its scent and colour; and it imparts to it its own nature and properties. Do the same to my soul by Communion, O Jesus! Thou descendest to my depths; thou, essential and uncreated life, makest divine the dust of my nothingness; and this nothingness, become divine, brings forth fruits worthy of thee—fruits of infinite price, because it is a divine sap which has made it fruitful. O Jesus, be thou my life, my holiness, my love!

I. BY HOLY COMMUNION WE ARE CLOSELY
UNITED TO JESUS CHRIST

"It is a union so close that Christ himself said to us.: *He that eateth my flesh and drinketh my blood abideth in me and I in him* : *my flesh is meat indeed, and my blood is drink indeed*; so that by Holy Communion the adorable Blood of Jesus Christ really flows in our veins, and his Flesh is truly mingled

with ours." [1]   We are united to his person,
his divinity, and his whole power, as food is
to our flesh.

Better still, after Communion the divinity
of Christ still dwells in our soul as heavenly
food; and the soul in its turn dwells in the
divinity of Christ as in an immortal and life-
giving food, or rather in the heart of life
itself; and this divine life ceases not to fill,
penetrate, and curb us by the influence of
habitual grace, holy inspirations, and good
impulses, the object of them all being to
transform us into Christ.

St Paul well expresses this union when he
says : *And I live, now not I, but Christ liveth
in me.* It is no more I who act and think,
but Christ who acts and thinks in me. O
unspeakable happiness! "No, only in heaven
shall we understand it. O my God, a creature
enriched with such a gift!"

"He who receives Jesus Christ in Holy
Communion," says St Cyril, "is so united to
him that they are like two pieces of melted
wax, which end by becoming one piece."

By Communion, indeed, Jesus Christ makes
us all his own body, and identifies us with
himself as the body with the head. He is
not content with showing himself to us. He
puts himself into our hands, into our mouth,
mingling his substance with our substance,
that we may become one spirit with him.

[1] Sermons, ii, 248 and 252.

II. THE EUCHARIST UNITES US TO JESUS CHRIST :
FIRST, BY INCREASING THE LOVE
OF GOD IN US.

"One Communion acts on the soul like bellows on a fire which has begun to go out, but where there are yet plenty of embers; we blow, and the hearth is lit up.

"One Communion well made is enough to inflame a soul with the love of God and make if forsake earthly things. A great man of the world came here not long ago to make his Communion. He had a fortune of £15,000. He gave £5,000 to build a church, £5,000 to the poor, and £5,000 to his relations, and he became a Trappist. After him came a very learned lawyer. He made a good Communion, and went off to place himself under the direction of Père Lacordaire. Oh! one Holy Communion, only one, is enough to disgust man with the world and give him a foretaste of heavenly delights.

"When you have received our Lord, you feel your soul purified, bathed in the love of God.

"When we have the good God in our hearts, they ought to be all aflame. The hearts of the disciples of Emmaus were on fire only to hear him.

"He who comes to Communion loses himself in God, as a drop of water in the ocean. They can be no more separated. It is no small thing, when you think of it, to be lost for eternity in that abyss of love.[1]

"After Communion the soul rests in the balm of love, as a bee among the flowers.

"What is it that our Lord does in the Sacrament of his love? He has assumed his kind Heart that he may love us, and there flows from that heart a stream of tenderness and mercy to drown the sins of the world.

"O Heart of Jesus! Heart of Love! Flower of Love! What should we love, if not the Heart of Jesus? There is nothing but love in that heart. How, then, can we help loving what is so love-worthy?"[2]

III. THE EUCHARIST UNITES US TO JESUS CHRIST : SECONDLY, BY INCREASING OUR LOVE FOR OUR NEIGHBOUR

Communion does indeed lavish upon us actual grace to love our brothers generously and sincerely. Do not suffer, then, ill-will or spite or hatred against your neighbour to be in your heart; that would be directly to counteract the action of Jesus within you. But that is not enough. At the time of Communion and afterwards, beg for the conversion of sinners, fervour for the lukewarm, health for the sick, and deliverance for the dead. When infinite love comes to you, it can refuse you nothing for the souls which are

[1] *Esprit*, 137-139; 350-351.   [2] *Vie*, ii, 417.

a thousand times more dear to it than to
yourselves. [1]

EXAMPLE

Of all God's creatures, the young man who
is attached to his (religious) duties is un-
questionably one of the most attractive and
lovable. By a privilege peculiar to his age,
he still preserves innocence while he already
has virtue. The affectionate feelings in which
his soul superabounds, concentrate themselves in God as in their source, falling in
streams of tenderness and devotion upon his
family, and thence spreading round him in
friendship, charity, and kindness. Respect
and confidence are in his look, and candour
in his smile. Thus appeared Jean-Marie
after his first Communion. He returned to
his own people, bringing in his heart and on
his face the sweetest impressions of boyhood.
His presence communicated calm and purity
to those who came near him. In his youth
everyone believed that Jesus Christ had taken
possession of him, that he animated and enlightened him, and that there was a constant
unity of spirit and desire between the God
of the Eucharist and his servant. François
Vianney, the witness of his life, delighted
to attest it. "After my brother's first Communion," he said, "his piety redoubled.
He edified not only our family, but the whole

[1] Sauvé, *Jésus intime*, iii. 58.

parish." Following Communions served only to strengthen these dispositions. Knowing that he must love his God alone, he never defiled the source of love in his heart. He passed without transition from ignorance of evil to the hatred of it; he was always an angel or a saint. "When I was young," he used to say, "I did not know evil; I have only learnt to know it in the confessional from the lips of sinners."

His sister Marguerite has given this testimony of him : "Our mother was so sure of obedience from Jean-Marie, that when one of us opposed or delayed to execute her orders, she had only to turn to my brother, who obeyed immediately, and then to hold him up as a model to us, saying : 'See if *he* complains, or hesitates, or murmurs. Why, he is off like a shot.' "

It is thus that the Holy Eucharist transformed Jean-Marie into our Lord.

O blessed Jean-Marie, pray for us, that each of our Communions may unite us so closely to Jesus Christ that nothing may be able to separate us from him : neither life nor death, neither the world, the flesh, nor the devil.

EIGHTH MEDITATION

THE EUCHARIST INCREASES SANCTI-FYING GRACE IN US

"WHEN Jesus entered the house of St Elizabeth, although he was imprisoned in Mary's womb, he sanctified both mother and child; and Elizabeth exclaimed, 'Whence comes so great a happiness to me, that the Mother of my God deigns to come to me?' I leave you to consider how much greater is the happiness of him who receives Jesus Christ in Holy Communion, not like Elizabeth, into his house, but into the depths of his heart, to be its protecting Master, not six months, as in Elizabeth's case, but all through life."

Oh, with what graces Jesus fills the soul that receives him with the dispositions of the holy precursor's mother!

I. HOLY COMMUNION INCREASES SANCTIFYING GRACE IN US.

"This is easy to understand, for in receiving Jesus Christ we receive the source of all kinds of spiritual blessings. We feel faith revive in us; we are more deeply imbued with the truths of our holy religion; we feel more keenly the greatness of sin and its dangers; the thought of judgement makes us more afraid, and the loss of God becomes more painful. In receiving Jesus Christ our spirit is strengthened; we are more steadfast in our combats; our intentions are purer in all we do, and our love is more and more enkindled. The thought that we possess Jesus Christ in our hearts, and the happiness we experience in that blessed moment, seem so to unite and bind us to God, that our heart can think of and desire nothing but God. We are so filled by the thought of the perfect possession of God that our life seems long : and we are envious, not of the long-lived, but of those who go early to their eternal reunion with God. We are gladdened by everything that reminds us of the destruction of our bodies."[1]

In increasing grace, the Eucharist enlightens our faith, revives our hope, kindles our charity, and sheds in our souls with a new profusion the gifts of Fortitude, the Fear of God, and Piety.

II. THE EFFECTS OF THE EUCHARIST ARE VISIBLE IN THE DEVOUT COMMUNICANT

"We can tell when a soul has received the Sacrament of the Eucharist worthily. It is so flooded with love, so pervaded and changed, that we recognize it no longer in its words and actions. It is humble, gentle, mortified, charitable, and modest, and at

[1] Sermons, ii, 249-250.

peace with everyone. It is a soul capable of the greatest sacrifices; in fact, it is unrecognizable. [1]

"St Magdalene of Pazzi tells us that it needs only one Communion, made with tender love and a very pure heart, to raise us to the highest perfection." [2]

"People who practise devotion, who confess and communicate often, and who neglect works of faith and charity, are like trees in blossom; you think there will be as much fruit as flower—but there is a great difference." [3]

EXAMPLE

One day, having just presided at the renewal of vows which the Sisters of St Joseph are accustomed to make each year on July 2, M. Vianney came from the ceremony, the joy which his full heart could not contain overflowing in delightful words. "How beautiful is religious life," he said, "how great is the multitude of thy kindness, O my God, to those who fear thee!... I was thinking just now that between our Lord and these good nuns, who are his spouses, there is a contest of generosity as to which should give the most. But our Lord always wins. The nuns give their hearts : *he* gives his Heart and his Body. While the nuns said, 'I renew my vows of poverty, chastity, and

[1] *Esprit*, 144. [2] Sermons, ii, 252.
[3] *Esprit*, 345.

obedience,' I said to them, giving them the Host, 'May the Body of our Lord keep your soul unto life eternal.' " [1]

The blessed Curé also contended with our Lord in generosity. Every morning he received the Body and Blood of Christ, and in return sacrificed his whole self in union with the divine Saviour. For the conversion of his parish he multiplied prayers, vigils, and scourgings, and led a life more and more austere. Insensible to so many mortifications, however, the people confided to his care indulged in dancing and frivolous pleasures with the same ardour, profaned the holy day of Sunday with the same obstinacy, and still frequented the public-houses. The holy Curé thought he was thus unsuccessful because he had not offered enough penances to our Lord, and he exclaimed, distressed but resolute," I will go on till I can do no more." It was then that he was found trying to live on the grass in his garden, and during certain periods of the year taking a meal only once every two days. And what a meal! It consisted of a piece of dry bread and a single boiled potato which was often mouldy. The servant of God was no less lavish towards souls with his time and toil than with his fasts and penances. In contact with the God of the Eucharist who delivered himself up for our redemption, and who daily renews

[1] *Vie.*

his sacrifice, M. Vianney's zeal was kindled to such a point that he could say one day : "If the good God should give me my choice of going to heaven this very minute or staying on earth till the end of the world to work for the conversion of sinners, I would stay, and I would continue to get up at midnight."

O blessed Jean-Marie, pray for us, that our Communions may render us stronger against the enemies of our salvation and against ourselves, purer and more mortified.

THE EUCHARIST WEAKENS OUR INCLINATION TO EVIL

"WE read in the Gospel that when Jesus Christ entered St Peter's house the saint prayed him to cure his mother-in-law, who was tormented with a violent fever. Jesus Christ commanded the fever to leave her, and at that instant she was cured so completely that she served them at table."[1]

The fever, says St Ambrose, is our avarice, anger, and voluptuousness. These passions eat into our very being, and agitate soul, mind, and senses.

They have their remedy in the Eucharist, *the corn of the elect, and wine springing forth virgins.*

Let us thank our Lord for this restoring and sanctifying gift.

I. "HOLY COMMUNION WEAKENS OUR INCLINATION TO EVIL"

"This is so true that when we have just received Jesus Christ we feel a new taste for heavenly things, and a new contempt for things created."[2]   There are two reasons for this : first, the living consciousness of Christ's presence, the pondered and grateful

[1] Sermons, ii, 245.   [2] *Ibid*, ii, 250-251.

memory of his visit, and the holy reverence and love with which it penetrates the soul, deter us from evil, and inspire us with a horror of it.

"How do you think pride can find entry into a heart which has just received a God humbled to annihilation? Can it willingly believe that it is anything of itself? On the contrary, will it not feel unable to humble and despise itself enough?

"Does not a heart which has just received a God who is so pure, who is holiness itself, feel born within it an invincible horror of all sins of impurity, and would it not be ready to be cut in pieces rather than consent to, I do not say a bad action, but even to a bad thought?

"When the mouth has been so happy as to hold its Creator and Saviour but a moment since, can it indeed dare to give itself to lascivious words or sensual kisses? No, undoubtedly it would never dare to do it.

"When the eyes have just now desired so eagerly to behold their Creator, who is purer than the sun's rays, could they indeed fix themselves after such a joy on anything immodest? It seems as though it were not possible.

"When a heart has just received in Holy Communion him to whom all things belong, and who passed his life in the greatest poverty, who had not where to lay his sacred head except on a handful of straw, and who died all naked upon a cross, do you think that heart could indeed be attached to the good things of this world, seeing how Jesus Christ behaved?

"Could a Christian who had just received Jesus Christ, put to death for his enemies, cherish hatred against those who have caused him pain? No; undoubtedly his pleasure will be to do them as much good as he can. [1]

"If we could comprehend all the good things contained in Holy Communion, nothing more would be wanting to content the heart of man. The miser would run no more after his treasures, or the ambitious after his glory; each would shake off the dust of earth, leave the world, and fly away towards heaven." [2]

II. Moreover, St Cyril says that the Eucharist, by kindling the ardours of charity in the soul, calms the disordered inclinations of our flesh, diminishes the fire of concupiscence, and strengthens our piety. It puts the devil to flight, so that he cannot excite our imagination or our senses by unwholesome images or dangerous impulses; it assures to us abundant graces, which remove occasions apt to awake our passions, and surrounds us with a special Providence. This is why St Bernard says, speaking to his monks: "If any one among you no longer

[1] *Sermons*, ii, 250-251.   [2] *Esprit*, 349.

feels violent assaults of anger, envy, lust, or other disordered desires, let him render thanks to the Body and Blood of Christ; it is the virtue of the Sacrament which is working in him."

Strengthened by the Eucharist, "one can no longer offend the good God; the soul is all embalmed with our Lord's precious Blood.... O beautiful life!"[1]

EXAMPLE

The Forty Hours' Adoration was being celebrated at Ars for the first time. The *grappin*[2] had that very morning set fire to M. Vianney's bed. At midday, when he went to see his missioner, he spoke to him of the Forty Hours, and the joys which the visible presence of the Holy Eucharist added to the ordinary charms of the pilgrimage. His eyes were full of tears, and his soul overflowed in every word. "It is another flame," said he, "and another fire.... It is a fire of love."

It was a fire which wholly consumed the natural imperfections of the man of God. M. Vianney had a strong inclination to make fun of things, for he had a keen eye and the power of repartee; but he never allowed any

---

[1] *Esprit*, 143.
[2] The "clutcher" or "grabber." The blessed Curé's half playful name for the devil, who showed his hatred of him by outward violences, to which various witnesses have testified.—*Translator*.

but kind words to fall from his lips, and he attained to the humble acceptance of reproaches which he had not merited. He was tempted against holy purity, and knew the humiliating buffets of which St Paul complains; but he preserved till his death the shining whiteness of the lily. He was born with an impetuous character, and he had to do himself extreme violence to acquire patience and gentleness. But he succeeded in this so well, that he could be crushed, stifled, or knocked down by the crowd without showing the least vexation, even in his looks. Did he not hold the Lamb of God in his hands each morning; was he not fed every day with the virginal Flesh of Christ; did he not steep his lips in the Blood of him who was on earth, says St Paul, *an image of* goodness? These sacred mysteries extinguished concupiscence in him, and made the grace of Jesus reign in his members.

O blessed Jean-Marie, pray for us, and obtain for us also grace to find in the Holy Communion the remedy for our evil inclinations, and the victory over our passions.

TENTH MEDITATION

THE EUCHARIST, PLEDGE OF ETERNAL LIFE AND SEED OF A GLORIOUS RESURRECTION

"WHY was Lazarus raised from the dead? Because he had often received our Lord into his house. The Saviour loved him so much that he shed tears at seeing him lifeless. How then should he leave in the humiliation of the tomb those whom he has honoured by his visit in Holy Communion, and who have eagerly desired him, and received him into a heart afire with love and clothed with purity? He has said : *I am the resurrection and the life. He that eateth my flesh and drinketh my blood hath everlasting life, and I will raise him up in the last day...*" [1]

HOLY COMMUNION IS A PLEDGE TO US OF ETERNAL LIFE

Thus it secures heaven for us : it is the earnest-money sent us by heaven to tell us that one day it will be our dwelling-place.

"Oh, if we could rightly understand how Jesus Christ loves to come into our heart! ... Once he is there he would wish never to go away; he cannot part from us again, either during life or after death..." [2]

---

[1] Sermons, ii, 245. [2] *Ibid.,* 251-252.

St Teresa appeared one day to a nun, in the company of Jesus Christ. "Why, O Jesus," asked the astonished nun, "dost thou accompany Teresa?" The Saviour answered that Teresa, during her life, had been so closely united to him in Holy Communion that he could not part from her!

"Oh! how beautiful a soul who has often and worthily received the good God will be in eternity! It will be united to the soul or our Lord. There it will rejoice with a pure and perfect happiness. It will shine like a beautiful jewel, because God will see himself in it.

"When the soul of a Christian who has received our Lord enters Paradise, it increases the joy of heaven. The angels and the Queen of angels come to meet it, because they recognize the Son of God in that soul.[1]

"Truly happy are they who receive Holy Communion at the hour of death. At the particular judgement which takes place directly after death, God the Father sees his Son in them, and he cannot condemn them to hell—oh no!...[2] The more often and the more worthily we have received him, so much the more glorious will be our bodies when raised by Christ. No, there are no actions which adorn our bodies for heaven better than Holy Communion.[3]

---

[1] *Esprit*, 141-143. [2] *Ibid.*, 148.
[3] Sermons, ii, 251-252.

"At the Day of Judgement our Lord's Body will shine through our glorified body, and his adorable Blood through our blood, as gold is seen shining in copper, or silver in lead." [1]

Can we doubt it, knowing how close is the union between Christ and the devout communicant?

If, then, Jesus Christ, when he was still passible and mortal, raised the dead by his touch alone, shall we not rise who eat his Flesh and drink his Blood? [2]

If a little yeast leavens the whole of a large lump of dough, if a spark suffices to set a house on fire, if one grain cast into the earth makes it fertile and produces others from it, how truly ought I to trust that thy blessed Body, entering into mine, in the fullness of time will raise it from corruption, kindle it with glory, and reproduce it immortal, impassible, agile, subtile, resplendent, and endowed with all the glorious qualities that can be hoped for. [3]

EXAMPLE

One day when the Blessed Sacrament was exposed, M. Vianney stood contemplating it with an ecstatic smile. One of his companions, surprising him in this attitude, turned his eyes instinctively towards the tabernacle as

[1] *Esprit*, 137-143.   [2] *Sermons*, 252.
[3] *St François de Sales*, III, 190-191.

though he expected to see something. He saw nothing, but the expression on M. Vianney's face had struck him so much that he said : "I believe the time will come when the Curé of Ars will live only by the Eucharist."

He was living by it already. The grace which flowed so abundantly from that Sacrament into his soul always protected him against sin, nourished in him the most magnificent virtues, and guided him without falling to the life of glory.

On Friday, July 29, 1859, having, as usual, spent sixteen or seventeen hours in the confessional, the holy curé came home worn out. He sank on to a chair, saying, "I can do no more." Then he went to bed never to rise from it again. Fear of God's judgements had been his dominant idea and despair his temptation; nevertheless, he was desirous of death, and looked forward to it with all his heart. "It is the union of the soul with the Sovereign Good," he said. And he passed his last days in perfect serenity. "I should not have believed," he delighted in repeating, "that it was so sweet to die."

On the Tuesday evening he himself asked for the Sacraments. He wept at hearing the bell which announced that Jesus was leaving the tabernacle to come and visit him, and he wept afresh on seeing him enter.

On Thursday, August 4, at two o'clock in the morning, he ceased to breathe, at the moment when the Abbé Monnin, who was saying the prayers for the commendation of the soul, pronounced these words : "May the holy angels of God come forth to meet him, and bring him into the city of the heavenly Jerusalem." Verily they brought him thither : the Church has given us the certainty of it by the decree of canonization of 1925.

And now the Eucharist will finish its work at the day of the blessed resurrection, for it has planted a seed of glory and eternal life in the holy priest's flesh. "Oh! how beautiful will be the Day of Resurrection!" he used sometimes to say; "those beautiful souls will be seen coming from heaven like glorious suns, to unite themselves to the bodies they animated on earth. The more those bodies have been mortified, the more they will shine like diamonds."

O blessed Jean-Marie, pray for us, that the Eucharist, food of our perseverance during this earthly life, may be our Viaticum at the supreme hour of death, and bring us to eternal glory.

THE EUCHARIST, SOURCE OF JOY

WHAT a happiness was the aged Simeon's when he was "pressing to his love-laden heart the child Jesus, who was enkindling and consuming that heart!" "Now, Lord, let me die," he cried out... Truly he was in ecstasy.

"But we, are we not happier than Simeon? *He* could keep Jesus only for an instant; we can keep him always, if we will. He comes not only into our arms, but into our heart."[1]

I. THE EUCHARIST, SOURCE OF SPIRITUAL JOY RESULTING FROM OUR LORD'S PRESENCE

"O my God, what joy for a Christian who has faith! On rising from the holy table he goes away with all heaven in his heart.[1]

"When we go to Holy Communion, we feel something extraordinary, a well-being which runs through the whole body from head to foot. What is this well-being? It is our Lord, who imparts himself to every part of our body, making it thrill with joy. We are compelled to say, like St John, *It is the Lord!* Those who feel nothing at all are much to be pitied!"[3]

"When you have had the happiness of

[1] *Esprit*, 205.   [2] Sermons, ii, 246.   [3] *Esprit*, 139.

receiving the good God, you feel for some time a gladness, a balm in your heart... Pure souls are always like that; and this union is their strength and happiness.

"O man, how happy you are, but how little you understand your happiness! If you understood it, you could not live... No, surely, you could not live.... You would die of love!... This God gives himself to you... you can take him away if you will ... where you will.... He is one with you!... Ah! a heart once clasped in the pure embrace of its Saviour could find no other happiness than in him."[1]

"One Easter Sunday, after Holy Communion, St Teresa was transported in God, and, returning to herself, was conscious of the Blood of Jesus Christ filling her mouth, which imparted to her such great sweetness that she thought she should die of love. 'I saw my divine Saviour,' she writes, 'who said to me : "My daughter, it is my will that this adorable Blood, which kindles such love in you, be for your salvation; never fear that my mercy will fail you. When I shed this precious Blood I felt only pain and bitterness; but to *you* it imparts only sweetness and love." ' Several times when she had the great happiness of communicating, a multitude of angels descended from heaven, and seemed to delight in joining with her to

[1] *Esprit*, 148.

praise the Saviour whom she carried in her heart." [1]

II. THE EUCHARIST, SOURCE OF SPIRITUAL SWEETNESS, WHICH IS SHED OVER OUR WHOLE LIFE

It is the happiness of feeling our strength renewed, our hunger appeased, and of being able to set about all the practices of the Christian life joyously and with fervour.

"Oh, how sweet a life is that life of union with the good God! It is heaven on earth; there are no more troubles, no more crosses." [2]

"Without the divine Eucharist there would be no happiness in this world; life would be unbearable. When we receive Holy Communion we receive our joy and happiness." [3]

" 'O my children,' the blessed Victoire used to say, 'why do you crawl along the way of salvation? Why have you so little courage to labour, and to merit the great happiness of taking your place at the holy table, and there eating the bread of angels which gives such strength to the weak? Oh! if you knew how this heavenly bread sweetens the miseries of life! Oh! if you had once tasted how good and kind is Jesus Christ to him who receives him in Holy Communion!... Go, my children, eat this bread of the strong, and you will return filled with joy and courage, desiring henceforth only sufferings, torments,

[1] Sermons, ii, 262.   [2] *Ibid.*, 147.   [3] *Ibid.*, 136.

and struggles, that you may please Jesus
Christ.' " [1]

EXAMPLE

M. Vianney loved to relate the story of
St John of the Cross and St Teresa when
they talked together of the joys of Communion : *the love of our Lord, going out from
one to the other, so melted their hearts that
St John sank down on one side (of the grille) and
St Teresa on the other, in the sweetness of love.*
... These words apply to no one better
than to the holy Curé of Ars. The Eucharist
was the refreshing "bath" in which, when
visited by temptations and trials, he loved to
plunge himself, and from which he came
forth strong and radiant.

It was the divine "flower" where, like
"the bees," as he expressed it, he rested with
delight, finding there a marvellous food,
a foretaste of paradise.

What tears of happiness he shed in celebrating holy Mass, and in holding our
Lord in his hands during his thanksgivings
and his long adorations.

This joy radiated over his whole life, and
made even crosses attractive to him. "I
have been much calumniated," he used to
say, "much gainsaid, and much knocked
about. Oh! I have had crosses; I have had
almost more of them than I could carry.

[1] Sermons, ii, 253.

Then I began to ask our Lord for the love of crosses, and I was happy. I said to myself, 'Truly, that is the only happiness.'" It was manifest on his face and in his conversation : this man, so stern to himself, was kind, gay, expansive; he knew how to smile; he could make pleasant speeches and had charming tact : the most tender and attractive expression rested on his lips, while truth and consolation fell from them. It stimulated and sustained his vigour, which he was never nearer recovering than at the hour when one saw him most worn out. The crowd, the heat, the obstruction, the length of time he sat in the holy tribunal—all that should have annihilated his strength—gave it back to him. In proportion as the necessities of the pilgrimage exacted, one saw him gain fresh strength, and rise superior to himself. It was because he drew a daily "renewal of youth," as the prophet expresses it, in the Blood of Jesus Christ, and in his burning colloquies with the God of the Eucharist.

O blessed Jean-Marie, pray for me, that Holy Communion may be my happiness too, and that, sustained by the Bread of Life, I may serve God joyously.

TWELFTH MEDITATION

SPIRITUAL DISPOSITIONS FOR COMMUNION—I

"WHEN Jesus Christ instituted the Eucharist, it was in a clean and well-furnished room, to show us what care we should take to adorn our souls with all kinds of virtues in order to receive Jesus Christ in Holy Communion."[1] Let us thank our Lord for this teaching.

The first adornment of the soul that would communicate is the state of grace, and next comes freedom from all affection for venial sin.

I. BEING IN A STATE OF GRACE IN ORDER TO COMMUNICATE WORTHILY

1. "We must be convinced, when we go to the holy table, that we have devoted all the necessary time to our self-examination, so as to have a thorough knowledge of our mortal sins," and that our confession has been full : and our minds must be firmly made up "to do, by God's grace, all that depends on ourselves to avoid falling again into sin. If we have been so unhappy as not to have accused ourselves fully of our faults, to have disguised or dissimulated some of them, in communicating we shall be placing Jesus Christ himself at the feet of the devil. What an enormity!

[1] Sermons, ii, 257.

"It is even good, says St John Chrysostom, before we have the happiness of receiving Jesus Christ into our hearts," to expiate our sins, "to weep over and do penance for them." There is something unfitting in approaching the holy table immediately after the confession of mortal sins.

2. "To communicate worthily, says St Bernard, we must do as the snake does when it wants to drink comfortably; in order that the water may do it good it relinquishes its venom. We must do the same. When we would receive Jesus Christ we must relinquish our venom, which is sin, the poison of our soul and of Jesus Christ; but we must relinquish it, this great saint tells us, for good and all. 'Oh! my children,' he says to us, 'do not poison Jesus Christ in our hearts.'

3. "Those who go to the holy table without having well purified their hearts, ought greatly to fear meeting with the same chastisement as the man who dared to sit down at the table without a wedding garment. The master commanded his servants to take him, to bind him hand and food, and to cast him out into the darkness. In the same way Jesus Christ will say at the hour of death to those who are so unhappy as to have received him into their hearts unconverted, 'Why have you had the boldness to receive me, when you were defiled with so many sins?' No, let us never forget that, to receive Communion, we must be

converted, and truly resolved to persevere."

"When we are going to receive the Body of Jesus Christ in Holy Communion, we must feel that we are in a fit state to die, and to appear with confidence before the tribunal of Jesus Christ."[1]

II. FREEDOM FROM AFFECTION TO VENIAL SIN, THAT WE MAY GATHER THE ABUNDANT FRUITS OF COMMUNION

"Before giving his adorable Body and his precious Blood, Jesus washed his Apostles' feet, to make us understand how necessary it is that we should be free from even the slightest sins. It is true that venial sin does not make our Communions unworthy, but it is the reason why we hardly profit by them. See, in fact, how you have made your communions : have you become the better for them? Perhaps not... Why? Because you nearly always cling to the same habits. You have a horror of gross sins which bring death to your soul; but as for all those impatiences, those murmurings, those little subterfuges in your speech, they scarcely trouble you. You will suffer nothing, and be contradicted in nothing, and you want everybody to love you and think well of you. You do not make the smallest effort to amend. Try and labour to destroy in yourself all that displeases Jesus Christ, and you will see how

[1] Sermons, ii, 256-258.

your Communions will make you walk with
great strides on your way to heaven; and the
more you do this, the more you will feel
yourself detached from sin and turned to God.
Look at St Teresa : she made worthy and
frequent Communions, and by this means she
became so pleasing to God, that one day
Jesus Christ appeared to her, and told her that
she pleased him so much, that if there were
no heaven he would create one for her alone. [1]

"So great is the purity of Jesus Christ that
the least venial sin prevents him from uniting
himself to us as entirely as he would.

"If we understood the value of Holy Communion we should avoid the slightest faults,
so as to have the happiness of receiving it
oftener. We should keep our souls always
pure in God's sight." [2] Yet more, we should
generously practise all virtues; "we should
not make any objection to speaking to those
who have given us pain, nor to seeing them,
nor to taking them into our inmost hearts..." [3]

EXAMPLE

Jean-Marie made his first confession one
night in 1796. The Revolution was in full
swing. His confessor, M. Groboz, attracted
by the vernal beauty of a life which had
blossomed in such purity in the midst of
storms, advised M. Vianney to place him at
Ecully, that he might there be prepared for

[1] Sermons, 258, 259. [2] *Esprit*, 142. [3] Sermons, ii, 257.

his first Communion under the immediate
and permanent influence of the missioners.

However, a year passed before this wish
was realized. A school was opened at Dardilly, and Jean-Marie's father sent him there.
His schoolfellows affirm that they were
accustomed to hear the good schoolmaster,
M. Thomas, say in order to spur them to
emulation : "Ah! if you were only like little
Vianney!" Study was a joy to the child, and
enabled him, little by little, to read the
catechism and the abridged version of the
lives of the saints. During the winter even-
ings he sat near the lamp and read aloud,
while the other members of the family, ranged
in a circle round the hearth, worked in silence
and listened to him.

After a year of hesitation, however, Mathieu
Vianney took his son to Ecully and entrusted
him to his aunt, Marguerite Beluse. The
energy of her convictions and the ardour of
her faith made her worthy of receiving this
trust. She encouraged her beloved nephew
in his devotional practices. She smiled at
his charity when, treating her like his mother,
he brought beggars home to her at night.

From the day of his instalment at Ecully,
Jean-Marie frequented the clandestine school
of Sister Combet and Sister Deville, two aged
nuns of St Charles. He made fragrant with
his piety both the school and the oratory
where he heard Mass. He was an object of

admiration for his mistresses themselves.

During the retreat preparatory to first Communion Jean-Marie was praying, lost in God, while the time passed unheeded, and he no longer felt the ground under his knees. "Look," said his companions, "look at little Vianney vying with his good angel!"

At last the hour came when that pure and limpid soul was opened to receive the Body and Blood of our Lord Jesus Christ. The first Communion took place in the Comte de Pingeon's house, during the small hours of the night, and behind windows sheltered by waggons of hay. The divine Spirit, the spirit of love and innocence, was revealed in the child's face. The real Presence of Jesus Christ was as sensible to him as that of his mother close by, and, when the Host was placed on his lips, an inexpressible joy wholly possessed him. So sweet a colloquy began between this virginal soul and its God, that, even after having renewed his baptismal vows, and made his consecration to the blessed Virgin, the child could not break it off. "My brother was so happy," declares Marguerite Vianney, "that he would not leave the room where he had received God for the first time."

O blessed Jean-Marie, pray for us, and obtain for us the grace to prepare ourselves like you for Holy Communion, by a great purity of life, by obedience, labour, and piety.

THIRTEENTH MEDITATION

SPIRITUAL DISPOSITIONS FOR COMMUNION—II

"Zaccheus, having heard of Jesus Christ, greatly desired to see him, and being hindered by the crowd, he climbed a tree.

"But the Lord, seeing him, said to him : *Zaccheus, come down, for this day I must abide at thy house.*

"Zaccheus hastened to descend, and ran to prepare all he could to receive the Saviour. On arriving, our Lord said : *This day is salvation come to this house.* Zaccheus, moved by the great charity of Jesus Christ, who had come to lodge with him, exclaimed : *Lord, I will give half my goods to the poor, and I will restore fourfold to all whom I have wronged.*"

O Jesus, give me the ardent desires of that sinner, his lively faith, and his joyous haste to receive thee; and coming into my heart, bring salvation to me also.

I. A GREAT DESIRE OF BEING UNITED TO JESUS CHRIST

"St Catherine of Genoa so hungered for this heavenly bread that she could not see it in the priest's hands without feeling as though she were dying of love, so great was her desire to possess it, and she would cry, 'Ah! Lord, come into me! My God, come to me, I can bear it no longer! Ah! my

God, come, if it please thee, into my inmost heart; no, my God, I can bear it no longer. Thou art my whole joy, my whole happiness, and the only food of my soul.'

"Happy the Christian who comprehends this. If we understood it even a little, we could only desire life so far as it meant the happiness of making Jesus Christ our daily bread. Created things would be nothing to us; we should despise them that we might cling to God alone. All we did and undertook would tend only to make us ever more worthy of receiving him." [1]

"When we cannot come to church, let us turn at least in the direction of the tabernacle. The good God has no walls to stop him. Let us say five Paters and Aves as a spiritual communion.... We can receive the good God only once a day; but a soul on fire with love makes up for that by the desire of receiving him at every moment.

"There is nothing so great as the Eucharist! Put all the good works in the world against one communion well made, and they are like a speck of dust beside a mountain." [2] How much, then, we ought to desire it!

II. A LIVELY FAITH

"This Sacrament being a mystery of faith, we must believe firmly that Jesus Christ is really present in the Holy Eucharist, and

[1] Sermons, ii, 253.　　　　[2] *Esprit,* 147.

that he is living and glorious there as in heaven. Formerly, before giving Holy Communion, the priest, holding the Holy Eucharist in his hands, used to say aloud : 'Believe, my brethren, that the adorable Body and precious Blood of Jesus Christ is truly in this Sacrament.' Then all the faithful replied : 'Yes, we believe it.'

"Oh! what happiness for a Christian to come and sit at the table of virgins and eat the bread of the strong!"[1]

III. A PURE INTENTION

"There are some who go to Communion to gain the world's esteem : that is no good. Others go from custom—sorry communions! They fail in purity of intention.

"Go to Communion to receive the graces which you need : humility, patience, purity ... go to the holy table to unite yourselves to Jesus Christ, that he may change you into other Christs. For if you communicate often and worthily, your thoughts, your desires, your actions, and all your undertakings will have the same end as those of Jesus Christ when he was on earth. You will love God, you will be touched by your neighbour's troubles, spiritual and temporal, and you will no think for a moment of attaching yourselves to eath; henceforth in heart and mind you will live only for heaven."[2]

[1] *Sermons*, ii, 261.   [2] *Ibid.*, ii, 260

"When you go to Holy Communion you must always have an intention, and say, when you are on the point of receiving our Lord's Body : 'O my good Father, who art in heaven, I offer thee, at this moment, thy dear Son, as he was taken down from the Cross and laid in the arms of the blessed Virgin, and offered by her to thee as a Sacrifice for us. I offer him to thee by the hands of Mary to obtain such and such a grace : faith, charity, humility....' My children, mark this well : whenever I obtained a grace, I asked it in this way, and it has never failed." [1]

EXAMPLE

To be living and efficacious, faith in the Eucharist should be enlightened. How can a soul receive the abundant graces of Communion, draw near to that venerable Sacrament with a profound and humble worship, and an ardent love for it, if that soul be unaware of the excellence and effects of the Sacrament, and ignorant of the dispositions of holiness which it demands? M. Vianney wished people to be instructed in everything concerning this Sacrament, as the following story bears witness :

Mme Maduel was one of those people occasionally met with, who are attracted to the holy table by a supernatural instinct which reveals the action of the Holy Spirit and the interior work of grace, but are un-

[1] *Esprit,* 132.

educated and possess little acquired knowledge. "Would you authorize me to communicate several times a week, Father?" she asked the holy curé. "Yes, my good soul," replied the servant of God. "But for your penance you must go to your curé and beg him to teach you the instructions of the catechism on Communion, and the dispositions one ought to bring to it." To avoid being catechized, the poor lady would willingly have renounced frequent Communion, but it was her *penance*! So she went to her curé's house and humbly begged him to instruct her. He, in order to spare his parishioner's susceptibilities, lent her two books—a catechism (Du Clot) and an ascetic author, showing her the chapters to read. She read them, and, on bringing back the two works, said to her curé : "I am very glad, all the same, to have had this penance, for I have learnt things of which I had no notion, and which will be very useful to me."

Her curé, M. l'Abbé Bernard, related this as a reply to those who reproached the Curé of Ars with knowing nothing of the direction of souls, and of favouring all the fantasies of false devotion.

O blessed Jean-Marie, pray for me, and obtain for me your ardent desires for Holy Communion, your faith, and your intentions, always so supernatural.

FOURTEENTH MEDITATION

UNWORTHY COMMUNION

UNWORTHY Communions are frequent. "How many have the temerity to approach the holy table with sins hidden and disguised in confession. How many have not that sorrow which the good God wants from them, and preserve a secret willingness to fall back into sin, and do not put forth all their exertions to amend. How many do not avoid the occasions of sin when they can, or preserve enmity in their hearts even at the holy table. If you have ever been in these dispositions in approaching Holy Communion, you have committed a sacrilege" — that horrible crime, on the malice of which we are going to meditate.

THE MALICE OF UNWORTHY COMMUNION

1. *It outrages God more than all other mortal sins.*

"It attacks the Person of Jesus Christ himself, instead of scorning only his commandments, like other mortal sins."

2. *Whoever communicates unworthily "crucifies Jesus Christ in his heart."*

He submits him to a death more ignominious and humiliating than that of the

Cross. On the Cross, indeed, Jesus Christ died voluntarily and for our redemption : "but here it is no longer so : he dies in spite of himself, and his death, far from being to our advantage, as it was the first time, turns to our woe by bringing upon us all kinds of chastisements both in this world and the next.

"The death of Jesus Christ on Calvary was violent and painful, but at least all nature seemed to bear witness to his pain. The least sensible of creatures appeared to be affected by it, and thus wishful to share the Saviour's sufferings. Here there is nothing of this : Jesus is insulted, outraged by a vile nothingness, and all keeps silence; everything appears insensible to his humiliations. May not this God of goodness justly complain, as on the tree of the Cross, that he is forsaken? My God, how can a Christian have the heart to go to the holy table with sin in his soul, there to put Jesus Christ to death?..."

3. *Unworthy Communion is a more criminal profanation than that of the holy places.*

"A pagan emperor, in hatred of Jesus Christ, placed infamous idols on Calvary and the holy sepulchre, and he believed that in doing this he could not carry further his fury against Jesus Christ. Ah! great God! Was that anything to be compared with the unworthy communicant? No, no! It is no longer among dumb and senseless idols that he sets his God, but in the midst, alas! of infamous living passions, which are so many executioners who crucify his Saviour. Alas! What shall I say? That poor wretch unites the Holy of Holies to a prostitute soul, and sells him to iniquity. Yes, that poor wretch plunges his God into a raging hell. Is it possible to conceive anything more dreadful?"

4. *Unworthy Communion is in certain respects a greater crime than the deicide of the Jews.*

"St Paul tells us that if the Jews had known Jesus Christ as the Saviour they would never have put him to suffering or death; but can *you*, my friend, be ignorant of him whom you are going to receive? If you do not bear it in mind, listen to the priest who cries aloud to you : *Behold the Lamb of God*; *behold him that taketh away the sins of the world*. He is holy and pure. If you are guilty, unhappy man, do not draw near; or else tremble, lest the thunders of heaven be hurled upon your criminal head to punish you and cast your soul into hell."

5. *Unworthy Communion imitates and renews the crime of Judas.*

The traitor, by a kiss of peace, delivered Jesus Christ to his enemies, but the unworthy communicant carries his cruel duplicity yet further. "Having lied to the Holy Ghost in

the tribunal of penance by hiding or dis-
guising some sin, he dares, this wretch, to
go with a hypocritical reverence on his face,
and place himself among the faithful destined
to eat this Bread.   Ah! no, nothing stops
this monster of ingratitude; he comes forward and is about to consummate his repro-
bation.   In vain that tender Saviour, seeing
that he is coming to him, cries from his
tabernacle, as to the perfidious Judas :
'Friend, whereto art thou come? What, thou
art about to betray thy God and Saviour
by a sign of peace? Stop, stop, my son; I
pray thee spare me!'   Neither the remorse
of his conscience nor the tender reproaches
made him by his God can stop his criminal
steps.   He steps forward.   He is going to
stab his God and Saviour.   O heavens! what
a horror! Can you indeed behold this wretched murderer of your Creator without
trembling?" [1]

EXAMPLE

Nothing grieved M. Vianney so much as
unworthy Communions and profanations of
the adorable Eucharist.   He never spoke of
them without sobbing; the sorrow he felt
was expressed in his tone of voice, in excla-
mations of atoning love, in the praises which
seemed to be a relief to that burning heart

[1] *Sermon sur la Communion indigne*, tome iv. *Sermons inédits.*

oppressed by grief. He had also appointed that Sundays and Thursdays should be consecrated by the orphans of his *Providence* to the work of reparative adoration. On those days the children stayed an hour in turn before the Blessed Sacrament to make reparation to our Lord. When they heard that a scandal had broken out somewhere, or that the glory of God's holy Name had been publicly and grievously outraged, the elder ones, who were the most fervent, asked their mistresses to let them spend the night in prayers. They relieved one another hour by hour, so that there was no interruption in the exercise of nocturnal adoration. How beautiful it was to see the piety of these poor children! At the school of St Jean-Marie they had learnt to conceive for sin the horror it deserves, and for our Lord the love which is his right. Nothing that affected him left them insensible.

O blessed Jean-Marie, pray for us and preserve us from the misery and crime of unworthy Communion.

FIFTEENTH MEDITATION

BODILY DISPOSITIONS
FOR COMMUNION

"COMMUNION!... Oh! how God honours his creature. He rests on his tongue, uses his palate as a pathway, and stays in his heart as upon a throne.[1]

Let your modesty be known to all men, in your dress, your looks, your attitude, your walk, *for the Lord is nigh.*[2]

To the dispositions of the soul necessary for a good Communion, the reverence due to the Sacrament requires that we should add certain bodily dispositions.

1. *We must be fasting.*

"We must not have swallowed anything by way of food or drink after midnight."[3] In a case of doubt it is more prudent to put off your Communion till another day.

2. *How we must be dressed.*

Our clothes need not be rich, but decent. It is impossible to "approve of girls" who

---

[1] *Esprit*, 349.   [2] *Phil.* 4. 5.
[3] Under the present (1959) regulations concerning the Eucharistic fast, solid food and alcoholic drinks may be taken up to three hours, and non-alcoholic drinks up to one hour before Holy Communion, and water can be taken at any time. — *Editor.*

make a "display of vanity in going to receive
a despised and humbled God : my God, my
God, what a contradiction!..." They seem
"to make no difference between the holy
table and a ball or dance."

It is also "wanting in reverence for Jesus
Christ" to communicate with clothes "torn
or dirty." See that they are clean. Change
your linen if you can : have your hair, face,
and hands in good order; the majesty of the
King of Glory, "who wishes to come into
our hearts," demands this much consideration
at least.

3. *Keep your body in perfect purity.*

"This Sacrament is called the bread of
angels to show us that, in order to receive it
worthily, we must come as near as we can to
the purity of the angels. The mouth that receives Christ, said St John Chrysostom, and
the body that enshrines him, ought to be
purer than the sun's rays."

4. *Your outward bearing.*

"This must announce to all who see you
that you are preparing yourself for some
great thing. Go to the holy table with great
modesty; be careful not to turn your head;
keep your eyes lowered and your hands
joined." [1]

[1] Sermons, ii, 254-255, 263.

EXAMPLE

There is nothing more admirable than the
contrast which existed between the poverty
of M. Vianney's house, clothes, and all be-
longing to his personal use, and the richness
of the sacred vessels and priestly vestments,
the neatness of the holy place, and of the
sacristy furniture.

The blessed Curé had found the house of
God in a state of complete destitution : he
resolved to decorate it. From the beginning
of his ministry he had several chapels made
in the church in honour of various saints.
Thanks to the help of generous benefactors,
he was able to acquire splendid vestments
and valuable sacred vessels, and he went
several times to buy them himself at Lyons.
His joy was unspeakable when he received
from the Vicomte d'Ars a magnificent canopy, superb chasubles, banners, a large
monstrance in silver gilt, a tabernacle of
gilded copper, some beautiful candlesticks,
and six reliquaries. The Count had bought
them for 40,000 francs. With the simplicity
of a child he invited his parishioners to come
and see these ornaments, showing his happiness and gratitude in a thousand ways.

When it was a question of objects destined
for divine worship, he could not find anything
beautiful enough. From M. Cabuchet, a
renowned artist, he ordered a splendid white

marble altar, which is to be seen today in the new church.

He sought, not exactly luxury, but whatever could procure the glory of God and stimulate the devotion of the faithful; everything in his church was decorated with such taste that it would have been difficult to find its equal in the country. He strove to celebrate the holy offices with all the splendour possible, especially on solemn feast-days. [1]

O blessed Jean-Marie, pray for us that we may always approach the venerable Sacrament of our altars with a holy reverence and religious modesty.

[1] *Sommaire.*

SIXTEENTH MEDITATION

THANKSGIVING

"WHEN we have communicated, if anyone said to us, 'What are you taking
home with you?' we might answer, 'I am
taking heaven.' One of the saints used to say
that we are 'God-bearers.'[1] It is quite true,
but we have not faith enough. We do not
comprehend our dignity. When leaving the
holy table, we are as blessed as the Magi would
have been if they could have taken away the
child Jesus."[2] Listen, then, after each of
your Communions, to our Lord, present in
your soul; talk to him; ask the blessed Virgin
to thank him for you, and remain all the day
in recollection. The most elementary proprie-
ty and our own interest make thanksgiving a
duty.

1. *After the happiness of communicating.*

"Rise modestly, return to your place, kneel
down, and do not immediately take up your
book or rosary.[3] I do not like to see people
begin to read directly they have come from
the holy table. Oh, no, what good are the
words of man when it is God who is speaking?...
We must be like someone who is very curious
and listens at the door. We must listen to all

[1] *Porte-Dieu*   [2] *Esprit,* 137.
[3] Sermons, ii, 263.

102

that the good God says at the door of our heart." [1]

2. *Talk for a little with Jesus Christ.*

"You have the happiness of possessing him in your heart, where he is in body and soul, as he was on earth during his mortal life. Ask him for all the graces you desire for yourself and others; the good God will be able to refuse you nothing if you offer him his Son and the merits of his holy death and passion." [2]

3. *Make your acts* [3] *after Communion.*

"Then invite the blessed Virgin and all the saints and angels to thank the good God with you. Do not go away directly after the holy Mass, but stay a moment to ask God to strengthen you well in your good resolutions." [4]

4. *On leaving the church.*

"Do not stop to talk; do not be dissipated, but, thinking of your happiness in bearing Jesus Christ within you, you must go home quickly and keep such guard over all your thoughts, words, and deeds that you may keep the grace of the good God all your life." [5]

"Take a vessel of cordial and seal it well, and you can preserve the cordial as long as you like. In the same way, if you keep our

[1] *Esprit*, 139.   [2] Sermons, ii, 264.
[3] *I.e., acts of faith*, etc.   [4] *Ibid.*
[5] Sermons, ii, 264.

Lord well by recollection after Communion, you will feel for a long time that devouring fire which inspires in your heart an inclination to good and a repugnance for evil." [1]

5. *How to spend any little time you may have between the services.*

"Use it in good reading, or a visit to the Blessed Sacrament to thank the good God for the grace he gave you in the morning. Talk of worldly matters as little as possible" [2] on the day of your Communion. [3]

EXAMPLE

During his first years at Ars, M. Vianney got up between one and two o'clock. He recited Matins and Lauds, betook himself to prayer, and about four o'clock sought the presence of the Blessed Sacrament, where he remained until seven; this was his preparation for Mass.

After the celebration of the sacred mysteries he began his thanksgiving, which lasted till midday. Have you seen the statue of St Jean-Marie on his knees? His body leans far forward, as though attracted by something invisible to all but him; his clasped hands

[1] *Esprit*, 138.   [2] *Ibid.*
[3] It must be remembered that the blessed Curé of Ars spoke these words to his parishioners, long before the papal decree of 1905 had declared the Church's wish to be that frequent and even daily Communion should be practised by the faithful of all ages and occupations.—*Translator.*

express the intensity of his feelings; his burning gaze, shining with joy, is fixed on the tabernacle; his smile is that of the Bride who beholds the Divine Beloved and delights in the possession of him : it is the attitude of ecstatic adoration. Such was the Curé of Ars kneeling on the altar steps, "bathing," as he said, "in the flames of love." If one of his parishioners wished to speak to him, he went out, and then, having briefly discussed the question submitted to him, he took leave of his interlocutor, excusing himself by saying : "Please excuse me, my friend; I must go back into the church, someone is waiting for me there."

O blessed Jean-Marie, pray for us that we may avoid all negligence in thanksgiving after Holy Communion, and may share your fervour.

SEVENTEENTH MEDITATION

THE REVERENCE DUE TO CHURCHES

HOW terrible is this place! this is no other but the house of God and the gate of heaven, exclaimed the patriarch Jacob, after the vision of the miraculous ladder. We can say as much of each of our churches; they are the dwelling of angels and archangels, the palace of God—heaven itself. If you do not believe it, look at the Table of the Sacrifice; remember for what cause and for what end it is erected; consider who it is that is going to descend upon it, and who will presently be offered there for you, and be pierced with a holy fear.[1]

1. "*Our temples are holy, reverend, and sacred.*"

"This is because a God made Man dwells there day and night.[2]...

"In olden times, many Christians crossed the seas to visit the holy places where the mystery of our redemption was wrought... 'Oh! happy places,' they exclaimed, 'where so many wonders were worked for our salvation!' But, without going so far, have we not Jesus Christ here in our midst, not only as God, but in body and soul? Are not our

[1] St John Chrysostom, I. *Ad. Cor.*, Hom. 36.
[2] Sermons, i, 383.

churches as worthy of reverence as the holy places? O happy Christian people, who daily see the renewal of all the wonders which God's omnipotence wrought of old on Calvary!"[1]

2. *Yet, "for the most part, we seem without reverence in our churches."*

"We seem to be without the love of God, without even knowing what we have come there to do. Some let a thousand earthly things occupy their mind and heart; to others, it is wearying and distasteful to be there; there are others who scarcely kneel down while God sheds his precious Blood for their pardon; others, finally, will scarcely let the priest come down from the Altar before they run away. My God, how little thy children love thee, or, rather, how they despise thee! In fact, what spirit is there of levity and dissipation which is not to be seen in church? Some are asleep, others talking, and hardly anyone is occupied with what he ought to be doing."[2]

3. *"It is faith that is wanting."*

"We are poor, blind beings with a cloud over our eyes. Faith alone can disperse that cloud...

"Because our Lord does not show himself in all his majesty in the most holy Sacrament, you behave yourselves here without rever-

---

[1] Sermons, i, 387. [2] *Ibid,.* ii, 131-132.

ence; but it is he notwithstanding!   He is
in the midst of you!... like that good bishop
who was there the other day; everybody
pushed against him...   Ah! if they had only
known that he was a bishop!...

"Presently, when I hold our Lord in my
hands, when the good God blesses you, ask
him then to open the eyes of your heart;
say to him, like the blind man of Jericho,
Lord, make me to see! You will surely obtain
what you desire, because he only wants your
happiness; his hands are full of graces which
he seeks to distribute, and, alas! nobody
wants them...   O indifference! Ingratitude!...
We are most miserable not to understand
these things! We shall understand them well
enough one day, but it will be too late!" [1]

EXAMPLE

St Jean-Marie displayed all the ingenuities
of priestly zeal to make his parishioners behave
reverently before the Blessed Sacrament during the services. He would have liked them to
keep to the habit of kneeling on the ground, and
deplored the use of a *prie-dieu* as a concession
to sensuality.   He never sat before the
Blessed Sacrament himself, unless the example of one of his superiors invited him to
do so.   Kneeling or standing was the only
position authorized, on the one hand, by his
faith in the presence of a "God so great and

[1] *Esprit,* 131, 61.

so awful," and, on the other, by the feeling of
his own unworthiness. Then nothing could
divert his gaze or his thoughts from our
Lord; he seemed no longer to see or hear
anything of what was happening round him.

"Did you know M. Vianney?" we were
asked one day by a pilgrim.— "No."—"I came
to Ars in August two consecutive years; it
was not long before his death. To see him
better, I placed myself in the stalls on the
epistle side, while he said Mass. At that
period of his life his eyes were slightly
bleared, and the flies had formed a sort of
circle round his eyes and were sucking his
blood. I watched attentively without taking
my eyes off the celebrant. During the whole
Mass he did not make the least sign, the
slightest movement of hand or head, to get
rid of these nuisances and remove that
suffering. What a man! what faith!"

O blessed Jean-Marie, pray for us that we
may always feel a profound reverence in the
presence of the divine Dweller in our taber-
nacles.

EIGHTEENTH MEDITATION

VISITS TO
THE BLESSED SACRAMENT—I

THE Spirit of the Lord is upon me, wherefore he hath anointed me to preach the gospel to the poor, he hath sent me to heal the contrite of heart, to preach deliverance to the captives, and sight to the blind, to set at liberty them that are bruised, to preach the acceptable year of the Lord, and the day of reward.[1]

These words which were uttered by thee, O Jesus, in the synagogue of Nazareth, ought to make thy tabernacle dear to me, for they speak to me of thy unceasing ministry there. Thou art always my Saviour, my light, and my physician.

I. THE INDIFFERENCE OF CHRISTIANS ABOUT VISITING OUR LORD IN THE MOST BLESSED SACRAMENT

"St Paul tells us that when he was in Athens he found written on an altar : *To the unknown God.* But I, alas! might say the contrary to you. I preach to you a God whom you do not adore, and whom you know to be your God. Alas! how many Christians are pressed for time, and only condescend to come for a few short moments

[1] St Luke 4. 18.

to visit their Saviour who burns with the desire to see them near him and to tell them that he loves them, and who wants to load them with blessings. Oh! what shame to us! If some novelty appears, men leave everything to run after it. But we run away from our God; and the time seems long in his holy presence! What a difference between the first Christians and ourselves! They passed whole days and nights in the churches, singing the praises of the Lord or weeping over their sins; but things are not the same today. Jesus is forsaken, abandoned by us" in the Sacrament of his love. [1]

II. THE SWEETNESS OF MAKING VISITS TO THE BLESSED SACRAMENT, AND MOTIVES FOR MAKING THEM

"If we really loved the good God, we should make it our joy and happiness to come and spend a few moments" before the tabernacle "to adore him, and ask him for the grace of forgiveness; and we should regard those moments as the happiest in our lives. Oh! how sweet and consoling are moments spent with the God of goodness. Are you in sorrow? Come and cast yourself at his feet and you will feel quite consoled. Are you despised by the world? Come here and you will find a good friend whose faithfulness will never fail you. Are you tempted?

[1] Sermons, ii, 131.

It is here that you will find strong and terrible weapons to vanquish your enemies. Do you fear the formidable judgement which has made the greatest saints tremble? Profit by the time in which your God is the God of mercies, and while it is so easy to win your pardon from him. Are you oppressed by poverty? Come here and you will find a God infinitely rich, and who will tell you that his wealth is yours, not in this world, but in the next. 'It is there that I am preparing for you infinite riches; go, despise the riches that perish, and you will have those that never decay.' " Sinners, "ask him with tears and sorrow for the pardon of your sins, and you are sure to obtain it." You who are reconciled with him, "beg for the precious gift of perseverance. Oh! tell him that if you are to offend him again, you would far rather die. Would you begin to taste the joy of the saints? Come here and you will know the happy beginnings of it.

"Ah! how good it is to enjoy the pure embraces of the Saviour! You have never tasted them! If you had had that happiness you could not leave them. Do not be surprised, then, that so many holy souls have spent their life, day and night, in his house; they could not tear themselves from his presence. We read the history of a holy priest who found such sweetness and consolation in our churches, that he slept on the altar step so as to have the happiness of finding himself near his God on waking; and God, to reward him, allowed him to die at the foot of the altar." [1]

EXAMPLE

"Go, my friend," M. Courbon had said, in appointing M. Vianney to Ars; "go, there is not much love of God in that parish; you will put it there." The love of God was, in fact, extinguished there in many souls; the passion for dancing and the public-house, and the profanation of the holy day of Sunday had stifled it. Who will ever know what the heart of the holy priest had to suffer from such a state of things? How much the uselessness of his ministry among the population where he was to spend his life must have filled him with sadness! That sorrow, however, never went as far as faint-heartedness. Fully recognizing the difficulty of the enterprise, M. Vianney believed that he would succeed by his prayers, sighs, and groanings before our Lord. From that time he resolved to consecrate his days and nights to entreating the divine mercy to act itself on the hearts of his parishioners, and he chose the church for his dwelling. He might be seen prostrate for long hours on the pavement of the choir, utterly motionless. There he recited a great part of his office, without any

[1] Sermons, ii, 137-138.

support whatsoever; his chest, wasted with fasting, heaved with long sighs; and he paused often, and gazed at the tabernacle with eyes wherein such vivid joy was portrayed, that one might have believed he saw our Lord, and which made his parishioners say : "Our curé is a saint." "I was truly struck with my spiritual wretchedness in the presence of God," a witness has testified, "when I beheld, by the light of the lamp which burnt before him, that spare, emaciated figure, and that shining gaze, riveted to the tabernacle with an expression of joy impossible to reproduce."

In his long prayers, the zealous Curé used to offer himself as a sacrifice for the conversion of sinners and to obtain in general the spiritual and temporal graces which he was begging from the divine goodness.

O blessed Jean-Marie, pray for us and win us grace to understand and to taste the fruits of visiting the Blessed Sacrament.

VISITS TO
THE BLESSED SACRAMENT—II

"WHEN you enter the church and take holy water, and when you raise your hand to your forehead to make the sign of the cross, look at the tabernacle. At the same time our Lord Jesus Christ opens it to bless you," and says to you, "Come to me, all you that are weary and sink under your burden, and I will refresh you."[1]

Thanks be to thee, O Jesus, for this word from thy kind heart. Oh! how sweet it is to hear it in the midst of life's dreariness and confusion! It illumines and rekindles my soul like a ray of sunlight.

I. WHY OUR LORD DWELLS IN THE MOST BLESSED SACRAMENT

"Our Lord is hidden there, waiting for us to come and visit him and ask him for what we want.

"He is there, in the Sacrament of his love, sighing and interceding unceasingly for sinners before God his Father.

"He is there to console us.

"To what outrages has he exposed himself that he might remain thus in the midst of us.

[1] *Esprit*, 128.

"See how good he is! He adapts himself to our weakness... In heaven, where we shall be triumphant and glorious, we shall see him in all his glory; if he had appeared before us now in all his glory, we should not have dared to approach him; but he hides himself like one in prison, saying to us, 'You do not see me, but that does not matter; ask me for all you want, and I will grant it you.' "

II. MOTIVES FOR VISITING THE BLESSED SACRAMENT, AND THE DELIGHTS FOUND THERE

"We ought to visit him often. How dear to him is a quarter of an hour spared from our occupations or from some useless employment, to come and pray to him, visit him, and console him for all the ingratitude he receives! When he sees pure souls hurrying to him, he smiles at them. They come with that simplicity which pleases him so much, to ask his pardon for all sinners, and for the insults of so many who are ungrateful.

"What happiness do we not feel in the presence of God, when we find ourselves alone at his feet, before the holy tabernacle! ... 'Come, my soul, redouble your ardour! You are here alone to adore your God! His look rests on you alone!' Ah! if we only had the angels' eyes! Seeing our Lord Jesus Christ here, on that altar, and looking at us, how we should love him! We should want to stay always at his feet; it would be a foretaste of heaven; everything else would become insipid to us." [1]

"It is like the good M. de Vidaud; he used to get up very early and go to adore the Blessed Sacrament as soon as the church was opened. Once when he was staying at a country house, they had to send three times to the chapel to fetch him to breakfast, and the mistress of the house was impatient. At the third summons, he left the presence of our Lord, saying 'My God, can I not stay quiet a moment with thee?' He had been there since four o'clock in the morning!... There are good Christians who would spend their whole life thus absorbed before the good God. Ah! how happy they are!" [2]

III. THE WAY TO MAKE A VISIT

"When we are before the Blessed Sacrament, instead of looking about us, let us shut our eyes and open our hearts; and the good God will open his. We will go to him, and he will come to us, the one to give, and the other to receive. It will be like a breath passing from one to the other. What delight we find in forgetting ourselves that we may seek God! [3]

"We need not speak so much to pray well. We know the good God is in the holy

[1] *Esprit*, 128-130   [2] *Ibid.*, 346.
[3] *Ibid.*, 134

tabernacle. We open our hearts to him, and delight in his holy presence; that is the best prayer. [1]

"It reminds me of the first time I came to Ars... Listen to this, my children : there was a man who never passed the church without entering it. In the morning when he went to work, and in the evening when he returned, he left his spade and his pickaxe at the door, and remained a long time in adoration before the Blessed Sacrament. Oh! I used to like that!... I asked him once what he said to our Lord during the long visits he paid him. Do you know what he answered? 'Oh, I don't say anything to him, Monsieur le Curé, I *look at* him and he *looks at* me...' How beautiful that is, my children, how beautiful that is!..." [2]

IV. PROLONG IT DURING THE NIGHT

"Listen, my children; when you wake in the night, transport yourselves in spirit before the tabernacle and say to our Lord : 'My God, here I am. I come to adore thee, praise thee, bless thee, thank thee, love thee, and keep thee company with the angels.... Say what prayers you know, and if you find it impossible to pray, hide behind your good angel and charge him to pray in your stead." [3]

[1] *Esprit*, 346.   [2] *Ibid.*, 134
[3] *Ibid.*, 130.

EXAMPLE

It sometimes happens during work in the fields that the labourer's tool gets broken or notched. As soon as the accident occurred at the Vianneys', they entrusted Jean-Marie, as the most nimble-footed, to take the damaged ploughshare or mattock to the village. Then Jean-Marie would spend all the time the blacksmith took in repairing them, on his knees before the Eucharist. Morning and evening, whenever he could, he went into the church going or returning from the fields, and stayed there, motionless, lost in the presence of our Lord. It is worth remarking that no one of his family ever complained about it, because he was the most strenuous at work and always the first at it. [1]

When he was curé, his first care was to arrange that our Lord should never be without adorers during the day. And he keenly exhorted his parishioners to give him daily this testimony of their love. His exhortations used to become more urgent during the Corpus Christi octave. "Our Lord is there on the altar," he would say to them, "ready to grant you all the graces you ask of him; you will surely obtain your conversion if you make it the object of your prayers! Come then, come, all of you! Twice a day the good God is going to bless you! O my God,

[1] *Annales d'Ars*, 1901-1902, 35.

what a pity it is that we are not moved by
thy holy presence!" He had made it a rule
that the girls from the *Providence* should make
a visit to the Blessed Sacrament every day.
From the first he gave active impetus to the
confraternity of the Blessed Sacrament; many
women and girls and about a fifth of the men
joined it.

"I have known people," said a witness at
the process for beatification, "who spent
their life, so to speak, in the church."

O blessed Jean-Marie, pray for me, and obtain me the grace like you to make visiting
the Blessed Sacrament my delight.

THE SENTIMENTS WITH WHICH WE OUGHT TO ASSIST AT THE CORPUS CHRISTI PROCESSION—I

" 'O CITY of Sion,' said the prophet, 'rejoice because your God dwells in the midst of you.' Words even more true for Christians than for Jews. Yes, Christians, rejoice! Your God is going to appear in your midst; this tender Saviour is going to visit your towns, your streets, and your houses; everywhere he is going to shed his most plenteous blessings. O happy houses before which he is going to pass! O happy roads beneath his holy and sacred footsteps!" [1]

"What is Jesus Christ doing when we carry him in procession? He is like a good king in the midst of his subjects, like a good father surrounded by his children, like a good shepherd visiting his sheep. [2] Let us accompany him with a lively faith, firm trust, and atoning love."

1. *With a lively faith and firm trust.*

"We should be like the first faithful who followed him when he was on earth doing good to everyone. Think of the two blind men who were on the Saviour's road, and

[1] *Sermons*, ii, 126.   [2] *Ibid.*, ii, 129.

began to cry, 'O Jesus, Son of David, have mercy on us.' Jesus restored their sight. Think of Zaccheus who, desiring to see Jesus in a procession, climbed a tree to look at him. Jesus converted him. Think of that poor woman afflicted for twelve years with an issue of blood, and who, in another procession, succeeded in touching Jesus : she was suddenly cured.

"If we had the same faith and trust we should win the same graces, for it is the same God, the same Saviour, and the same Father, moved by the same charity. Alas! how many sick to cure, how many blind to whom sight must be given! How many Christians who are going to follow Jesus Christ with their poor souls all covered with wounds! How many Christians who are in darkness and do not see that they are ready to fall into hell! My God! cure these and enlighten those! Poor souls, how wretched you are!" [1]

2. *With atoning love.*

"Let us imagine, in this procession, the Saviour going to Calvary : some were kicking him, others loading him with abuse and blasphemies.... Only a few holy souls followed him, weeping and mingling their tears with his precious Blood with which he was sprinkling the paving-stones.

"Oh! how many Jews and executioners

[1] Sermons, ii, 129-130.

are about to follow Jesus Christ, and who are
not content with putting him to death once"
by mortal sin, "but will slay him on as many
altars as they have hearts!   Of how many
profanations, of how many sacrileges has he
been the object during this long procession
of nineteen centuries, from the institution of
the Eucharist to this day!   Ah! is it possible
that a God who loves us so much should be
so despised and malreated?"[1]

"Let us be like one friend sorrowing over
the misfortunes of another and thus showing
him true friendship : let us grieve over the
contempt cast upon Jesus Christ, and try to
make amends for it by a greater and more
ardent love."[2]

EXAMPLE

M. de la Forte, M. Gaston de Bon-Repos,
MM. Anthelme and Henri des Garets were
carrying the canopy in a procession of the
Blessed Sacrament.   It was one of the later
years of the holy Curé's life.   The procession
stretched along the road from the church
to the château, and M. le Curé staggered
under the weight of the monstrance, swaying
now to the right, now to the left. He kept his
eyes fixed continually on the sacred Host,
and he shed copious tears; from the château
to the church his tears did not cease to flow,
and were raining on to his cope.   At every

[1] Sermons, 135-136.   [2] *Ibid.*, 132.

moment the bearers feared he would fall. On
the return of the procession, which had been
very long, his asistant priest wanted to make
him take some refreshment.   He refused it,
saying : "It is needless; I don't want anything.
How could I be tired? He whom I carried was
carrying me also." It was indeed the observa-
tion that each one had made, and twenty
times in the course of the procession one had
wondered by what miracle blessed Jean-Marie
kept on his feet.

O blessed Jean-Marie, pray for us; obtain
that we may walk in Jesus' train with that
faith, hope, and charity which opened to you
the heart of the divine Master and the treasury
of his graces.

THE SENTIMENTS WITH WHICH WE OUGHT TO ASSIST AT THE CORPUS CHRISTI PROCESSION—II

"WHAT a consoling day is this for us! This alien earth will presently become verily the image of the heavenly Jerusalem. The feasting and joys of heaven will come down to earth." Jesus will pass through the streets of our city! "When we pass by this road again, how can we help saying to ourselves : 'This is where my God passed by, here is the path he took when he was scattering his benedictions through this parish. Oh! if my tongue can forget his benefits, may it cleave to the roof of my mouth!... Oh! if my eyes should turn their gaze again to earthly things, may heaven refuse them light!' " [1]

That we may gather the graces Jesus offers us on this glorious day, let us follow him with submissive attention to his words, with the deepest reverence, with a joy wholly celestial.

I. WITH SUBMISSIVE ATTENTION TO HIS WORDS

"We read in the Gospel how the two disciples of Emmaus walked with the Saviour without knowing him, and how, when they recognized him, he disappeared. Transported

[1] Sermons, ii.

by their happiness, they said one to another, 'Did not our hearts seem all on fire with love when he spoke and explained the Scriptures to us?' We, a thousand times happier than those disciples who walked with Jesus Christ without recognizing him, know that it is our God and Saviour who walks before us, who will presently speak in the depths of our hearts, and who will inspire in them numberless good thoughts and inspirations. 'My son,' he will say, 'why will you not love me? Why will you not forsake that accursed sin which puts a wall of separation between us? Oh! my son, can you verily abandon me? Will you indeed force me to condemn you to eternal torments? My son, here is your pardon; will you repent!' Or perhaps he will urge us to a love more filial, more tender, and more generous."[1] Let us listen to him.

II. WITH THE DEEPEST REVERENCE

"Let us remember that we are sinners unworthy to follow so pure and holy a God."[2]

"It is quite certain that if we had the happiness of so many of the saints to whom God has revealed himself—sometimes as a child in his crib, sometimes on the Cross—we should indeed be moved to the greatest reverence for him. But he is no less present in the midst of us, under the veils of his Sacrament.[1]

[1] *Sermons*, ii, 134.   [2] *Ibid.*, 129.   [3] *Ibid.*, 135.

"When the ark of the Lord passed over the land of the Bethsamites, fifty thousand among them were struck dead, because they had been wanting in reverence! How that example ought to make us tremble! What was enclosed in the ark? A little manna, and the tables of the law; and because those who approach it are not sufficiently impressed by his presence, the Lord strikes them dead. But who is he that, reflecting even for a moment on the presence of Jesus Christ, will not be seized with fear?" He is the true manna which came down from heaven, the living bread of our souls, the sovereign law-giver, the all-powerful and all-holy God!

Would it not be supreme disrespect to follow him in dissipation, with a heedless mind and a sullied heart? "How many are actually miserable enough to walk in the company of the Saviour with a heart which is *full of sins*. In vain will you bend the knee, O most miserable, when God is uplifted to bless his people. His piercing gaze will not fail to see the horrors which are passing in your heart."[1]

III. WITH A JOY WHOLLY CELESTIAL

"Let us imagine the great day of that procession which will take place after the general judgement." Today, he invites us to win heaven and become worthy of it; then, he

[1] Sermons, ii, 133.

he will lead us in thither himself, and we shall take part in the glorious procession of the elect. Now, he is hidden from our eyes under the humility of his Sacrament, to try our faith; then, he will walk, clothed with majesty, light, and power, at the head of his saints, whom he will satiate with his glory. Now, our procession is made among the suffering and miseries of this life, in the train of a crucified God who wills that we should bear our cross with him; then, the tears of all the bruised and persecuted will be changed into a canticle of joy and eternal mirth.

EXAMPLE

St Jean-Marie loved the feast of the Most Blessed Sacrament best of all. The procession of that day was one of his consolations. When he announced it, "it seemed as though his heart were flooded with love and tenderness for our Lord; and he prepared for it with the keenest solicitude and display of all the splendour possible. He took care that beautiful altars of repose were set up along the roads and richly decorated, and he multiplied them so as to multiply the benedictions. He went from one to another, encouraging, with a kind remark or with words of burning faith, those who were decorating. When the hour for Mass approached, wanting to see for himself that the choir-boyswere ready and decently dressed, he would enter a room of the old presbytery and say smiling, with a satisfied air, 'Ah, my children, if your souls were as white as your surplices, how pleased our Lord would be.'

"Then, robed in sumptuous vestments, he himself carried the Blessed Sacrament in the procession, with a faith and love which was written so plainly in his face and aspect, that it was impossible to witness it without feeling a deep and sanctifying impression." [1]

O blessed Jean-Marie, pray for me that I may become worthy, by the innocence and sanctity of my life, to take part in the great procession of the virgins in heaven, who *follow the Lamb whithersoever he goeth.*

[1] *Sommaire.*

TWENTY-SECOND MEDITATION

ON THE PRIEST

"MARVELLOUS dignity of priests!" exclaims St Augustine; "in their hands, as in the womb of the blessed Virgin Mary, the Son of God becomes incarnate." *They are the ministers of Christ and dispensers of the mysteries of God*, St Paul had said before him. Commenting on these words, the Curé of Ars said, in his turn, "Without the priest the death and passion of our Lord would be no use; the priest has the key of the heavenly treasures; he is God's steward and the administrator of his goods." Let us ask the Holy Ghost to give us knowledge of these truths. It will inspire us with a religious veneration for the character of the priest, and a lively gratitude towards our Lord who has invested him with it.

I. THE PRIEST'S GREATNESS

"What is the priest? A man who holds the place of God, a man clothed with all the powers of God. *Go*, our Lord said to the priest, *As my Father hath sent me, I also send you.*

"At the consecration the priest does not say, 'This is the Body of our Lord.' He says, '*This is my Body.*'

"Behold the power of the priest! The tongue of the priest makes God from a morsel of bread! It is more than creating the world. Someone said, 'Does St Philomena, then, obey the Curé of Ars?' Certainly, she may well obey him, since God obeys him. The blessed Virgin cannot make her divine Son descend into the host. A priest can, however simple he may be.

"How great is the priest! He will only rightly understand himself in heaven... To understand it on earth would make one die, not of fear, but of love...

"If I were to meet a priest and an angel, I should salute the priest before the angel. The latter is the friend of God, but the priest stands in his place. St Teresa used to kiss the ground where a priest had passed.

"Great value is attached to objects which have been laid in the porringer of the blessed Virgin and the child Jesus at Loreto. But the fingers of the priest which have touched the adorable Flesh of Jesus Christ, been dipped in the chalice which has held his Blood, and in the ciborium which has held his Body—are they not more precious?...'

II. THE PRIEST THE NURSING-FATHER OF SOULS
AND THE PILLAR OF RELIGION

"When the bell summons you to church, if you were asked : 'Where are you going?' you might answer, 'I am going to feed my

soul!' And if someone pointed to the tabernacle and asked you, 'What is that gilded
door?' 'It is the store-cupboard—my soul's
store-cupboard.'[1] 'Who has the key? Who
provides everything? Who makes ready the
feast, and waits at table?' 'The priest.'
'And the food?' 'It is the precious Body and
Blood of our Lord.'... O my God, my God!
how thou hast loved us!''[2]

"The priest is to you as a mother, as a
nurse to a baby. She gives him his food;
he has only to open his mouth. 'There, my
little one, eat,' the mother says to her child.
'Take and eat,' the priest says to you; 'this
is the Body of Jesus Christ; may it keep you
and bring you to eternal life!' O glorious
words!... A child rushes to his mother
when he sees her; he struggles with those
who hold him back; he opens his little mouth
and stretches out his little hands to kiss and
clasp her. So in the presence of the priest your
soul springs naturally towards him; it runs to
meet him, but is held back by the bonds of the
flesh in men who give all to the senses and live
only for the body."[3]

"At sight of a spire you may say, 'What is
there? The Body of our Lord. Why is it
there? Because a priest has been there and
has said holy Mass.'

"The priest is everything, after God!...

---

[1] *Garde-manger*, literally "larder."   [2] *Esprit*, 116 *et seq.*
[3] *Cadavre*, literally "corpse, dead body." *Esprit*, 50.

Leave a parish for twenty years without a priest, and beasts will be worshipped there.

"If M. le Missionaire and I were to go away, you would say, 'What is there to do in that church? There is no more Mass. Our Lord is no longer there; we may just as well pray at home...'

"When men want to destroy religion they begin by attacking the priest, because where the priest is no more, there is no more sacrifice, and where there is no more sacrifice, there is no more religion.

"The priesthood is the love of the heart of Jesus. When you see the priest, think of our Lord Jesus Christ."

EXAMPLE

M. Vianney once said at catechism : "To celebrate Mass one ought to be a seraph! I hold our Lord in my hands. I move him to the right, and he stays there, to the left, and he stays there!... To know what the Mass is would be to die. Only in heaven shall we understand the happiness of saying Mass!... Alas, my God! how much a priest is to be pitied when he does this as an ordinary thing!...

St Jean-Marie showed great reverence for the sacred liturgy, and observed its least details with much exactness. When he distributed Holy Communion his face lit up and wore an angelic expression; his voice was

full of deep emotion, and tears of love often
fell from his eyes.

O blessed Jean-Marie, blessed be God for
having given you to the world to teach it in
your person what the priest is, his high dignity and his beneficent power! Make us
always to venerate our priests as the dispensers of God's mysteries and the ministers
of him who *went about doing good*.

THE HOLY SACRIFICE OF THE MASS

FROM *the rising of the sun even to the going down, my name is great among the Gentiles, and in every place there is sacrifice, and there is offered to my name a clean oblation : for my name is great among the Gentiles, saith the Lord of hosts.*[1]   The world, in fact, since the redemption, is an immense temple where at each moment of time, as the sun advances over a hemisphere, the victim of Calvary is uplifted between heaven and earth by thousands of priests, to the glory of the Most High.   Victim essentially immaculate, who keeps his sanctifying virtue even when he is offered by unworthy hands, Jesus substitutes himself for guilty men, to give to the Father the honour his Sovereign Majesty demands, and to implore his mercy and graces on their behalf.

I. ITS NATURE

"The main point of the holy Mass is in the words of consecration.[2]   How glorious it is!   After the consecration, the good God is there as in heaven!...   If man really understood this mystery, he would die of love.   God spares us because of our weakness.[3]

"The holy sacrifice is the same as that of the Cross, which was offered once upon Calvary, on Good Friday.   The only difference

---

[1] Malachias I. II.   [2] Sermons, ii, 145.   [3] *Esprit*, 125.

is that, when Jesus Christ offered himself on Calvary, the sacrifice was visible; that is to say, Jesus Christ was seen with the bodily eyes, being offered to God, his Father, by the hands of his executioners, and shedding his Blood : it means that the Blood came forth from his veins and was seen flowing down upon the ground. But in the holy Mass, Jesus Christ offers himself to his Father in an invisible and unbloody manner."

II. ITS NECESSITY AND ITS ENDS

"Man, as a creature, owes to God the homage of his whole being, and as a sinner he owes him an atoning victim; that is why, in the ancient law, multitudes of victims were daily offered to God in the temple. But those victims could not make entire satisfaction to God for our sins; it needed another, holier and purer, who was to continue to immolate himself to the end of the world, and who was capable of paying what we owe to God. That holy Victim is Jesus Christ himself, who is God like his Father, and man like ourselves. Every day he offers himself on the altars, as once on Calvary.

"By this pure and stainless oblation, our Lord renders to God all the honour due to him, and acquits himself, for man, of all that man owes to his Creator; he immolates himself each day in acknowledgement of God's sovereign dominion over his creatures, and

the outrage given to God by sin is fully
repaired. Being the mediator between God
and man, all the graces we need he obtains
for us by this sacrifice; and being made like-
wise the victim of thank-offering, he renders
to God, for men, all the gratitude they owe
him." [1]

III. ITS VALUE AND FRUITS

"If you want an idea of the greatness of
merit in the holy Mass, it suffices for me to
tell you, with St John Chrysostom, that it
rejoices the whole court of heaven, relieves
the poor souls in purgatory, brings all manner
of blessings upon the world, and gives more
glory to God than the sufferings of all the
martyrs, the penance of all solitaries, and
all the tears they have shed since the beginning of the world, and will do till the end
of the ages. The reason is clear. All these
actions are done by sinners more or less
guilty, while in the holy sacrifice of the Mass
it is a man-God, equal to his Father, who
offers him the merit of his death and passion. [2]
All these works are the works of men, and
the Mass is the work of God; martyrdom is
the sacrifice man makes of his life to God,
and the Mass is the sacrifice of his Body and
Blood which God makes to man. [3]

"You see from this that the holy Mass is of
infinite value. Let us notice, too, in the
Gospel, that at the moment of Christ's death,

[1] Sermons, ii, 141.   [2] *Ibid.*, ii, 142.   [3] *Esprit*, 123.

many conversions were wrought; the good thief received the promise of paradise, many Jews were converted, and the Gentiles struck their breasts, saying that he was indeed the son of God; the dead arose, the rocks were rent, and the earth trembled."[1]

EXAMPLE

The belief that the holy Curé saw our Lord on the altar, that he beheld him with his eyes, that he knew him "in the breaking of bread," came to all who were fortunate enough to assist at his Mass. It was impossible to behold a face more expressive of adoration, or more illumined with that heavenly radiance which manifests the working of the Holy Ghost. It seemed as though a ray of divine glory fell upon him. Heart, mind, soul, and senses seemed alike absorbed, and so indeed they were. One could not discern a moment's distraction in his prayer. In the midst of the crowd and under the influence of so many eyes fixed upon him, he held communication with our Lord as freely as though he had been in the solitude of his poor room. He shed tears of love in his presence. Usually his tears were not dry all the time the holy mysteries lasted.

O blessed Jean-Marie, pray for us and obtain us grace to be quickened, during the holy Mass, by the fervour with which you celebrated it each day.

[1] Sermons, ii, 142.

DAILY MASS

You *shall draw waters with joy out of the Saviour's fountains :* [1] mysterious, life-giving waters of grace, of conversion for sinners, perseverance and sanctity for the just, refreshment, light, and peace for the faithful dead. These waters spring from all the wounds of the Saviour hanging on the Cross. Just as Moses, by striking the rock in the desert, caused a fountain of living water to flow from it, where the Hebrews quenched their thirst; so the thorns and nails that pierced Christ's flesh, and the whips that tore it, have opened to Christian souls an inexhaustible fountain of graces which the holy Mass distributes to them according to their desires and their devotion. Happy are those who assist often and with devotion at the holy sacrifice; they will enrich themselves and their brethren with all God's gifts. Daily Mass is the channel of the most precious and abundant graces.

I. THE GRACE OF CONVERSION

"Do you want to bring about a change in your life—that is to say, to leave sin that you may come back to the good God? Hear

[1] Isaias 7. 3.

some Masses for that intention, and if you hear them devoutly you may be sure that the good God will help you to leave sin, even were you so wretched as to be obstinate as the Jews, blinder than the Gentiles, and harder than the rocks that were rent at the death of Christ.   Here is an instance of it. The story is told of a girl who had led a most wretched life for several years.   All at once, considering the state of her poor soul, she felt seized with terror.   Directly after Mass she went to a priest to pray him to help her to leave sin.   The priest, who knew her life, asked her what had wrought such a change in her. 'Father,' she said, 'during the holy Mass, which my mother before her death made me promise to hear every Saturday, I conceived so great a horror of my condition that I can bear it no longer.'   'O my God!' exclaimed the priest, 'here is a soul saved by the merit of the holy Mass.'   Well, then, may the Council of Trent say that the Mass appeases the anger of God and converts sinners." [1]

II. MANIFOLD GRACES OF SALVATION

"St Thomas says that one day during holy Mass he saw Jesus Christ with his hands full of treasures which he was seeking to distribute, and that if we were so happy as to attend Mass often and holily, we should

[1] *Sermons*, ii, 143, 156-158.

have many more graces than we possess for our soul's salvation and even in temporal things." [1]

"St John Chrysostom has said that there is no time in which to treat with God of our salvation, more valuable than that of holy Mass, where Jesus Christ offers himself as a sacrifice to his Father to procure us all kinds of blessings and graces. Are we in affliction? says this great saint : we shall find all manner of consolation at Mass. Are we tempted? Let us hear holy Mass, and we shall find there a way of overcoming the devil.

"Pope Pius II relates that a gentleman of the district of Ostia, being continually combated by a temptation to despair, went to a holy monk to show him the state of his soul. The monk advised him to have a priest in his house, who would say Mass for him every day. The gentleman followed this advice; every day a priest said Mass for him, which he attended as devoutly as he could. He obtained by this means great peace of mind. And at the hour of death he declared that since he had had the happiness of attending the holy sacrifice every day the devil had no more tempted him to despair." [2] If we had enough faith, the holy Mass would be a remedy for all our ills, for Jesus Christ is the physician of soul and body.

[1] *Sermons,* 152.   [2] *Ibid.,* ii, 143-145.

III. THE GRACE OF A GOOD DEATH

" 'Know, my daughter,' said Jesus Christ to St Mechtilde, 'that the saints will attend the death of all those who have heard holy Mass devoutly, to help them to die well, to defend them against the temptations of the devil, and to offer their souls to my Father.' What a blessing for us to be helped and attended at that dreadful moment by as many saints as we have heard Masses!" [1]

IV GRACES OF DELIVERANCE FROM PURGATORY

"After the consecration God fixes his eyes upon the altar : 'There is my beloved Son,' he says, 'in whom I am well pleased.' To the merits of the offering of that Victim he can refuse nothing. You remember the story of the holy priest who prayed for his friend who, as God had apparently made known to him, was in purgatory. There came to him the thought that he could do nothing better than offer the holy sacrifice of the Mass for his soul; and at the moment of the consecration he took the host in his hands and said, 'Holy and eternal Father, let us make an exchange. Thou holdest the soul of my friend, which is in purgatory, and *I* hold the Body of thy Son, which is in my hands. Well, deliver my friend, and I offer

[1] Sermons, 153.

thee thy Son with all the merits of his death and passion.' And, indeed, at the moment of the elevation he saw the soul of his friend going up to heaven all radiant with glory." [1]

EXAMPLE

The Curé of Ars used to say that during the Revolution, as soon as it was known that the sacred mysteries were to be celebrated somewhere, everyone exclaimed : "There is a Mass there; let us go." All went to it, but no one resorted there as often as he, and nobody participated as he did in that act, the most sublime and the most necessary of all Christianity. Nothing was talked about but the piety of young Vianney.

When the Concordat had restored liberty to the Church, and Jean-Marie could attend Mass at Dardilly itself, he would have wished to hear it every day. Work in the fields, in which he was employed from his thirteenth to his nineteenth year, did not allow him to follow his attraction; and he was one of those who concede their holiest desires to the duties of their state of life, for he thought a day spent in obedience by tilling the ground was "more pleasing to God than a day spent of his own free will before the tabernacle."

But this discretion, so rare at his age, was not opposed to the seizing of every opportunity that occurred to satisfy a devotion ever

[1] *Esprit*, 127-128.

unsatiated. His father suffered from rheuma-
tism, and seeing him helpless, the young
man said to him affectionately : "Let me go
to Mass, and I will say so many *Paters* and
Aves that your pains simply must cease."
And M. Vianney yielded to such winning
entreaties.

If dawn found Jean-Marie in the vineyards
or the plough-field, as soon as he heard the
bell ring for Mass, he said five *Paters* and five
Aves, and formed in his heart an eager desire
to receive the Body and Blood of Jesus Christ.
At Nöes he was at Mass nearly every morning
of the week.

O blessed Jean-Marie, pray for us that,
taught by your example and precepts, we
may love to be at holy Mass every day.

OBJECTIONS TO DAILY MASS

I HAVE *spread forth my hands all the day to an unbelieving people who gainsaid me.*[1] It is our Lord's complaint at sight of the indifference of men for the holy sacrifice of the Mass and the work of redemption. Jesus has spread forth his hands on the Cross to embrace us all in the intensity of his charity, and overwhelm us with the graces of his mercy—the last and supreme effort of a God dying in the midst of unspeakable sufferings. Ought we not to be moved to tears by so much love, and to have recourse each day to the holy sacrifice of the Mass, which renews that of the Cross? Alas! an altogether worldly wisdom, human respect, and an unworthy preference accorded to the things of time over those of eternity keep us back. Let us make amends to our Lord for this indifference, and try to understand that nothing can excuse it.

I. DO NOT BE AFRAID THAT HOLY MASS WILL HINDER YOU IN YOUR BUSINESS

"It is quite otherwise. Be sure that all will go better, and that your business will succeed better than if you have the mis-

[1] Isaias 65. 2.

fortune not to attend it... Alas! if we put all
our trust in God, how much happier we
should be! But, you say to me, if we have
nothing, we shall be given nothing. What do
you expect the good God to give you when you
rely only on your work, and not at all on him?
since you only take time to say your morning
and night prayers, and content yourselves
with coming to Mass once a week. You do
not know the resources of the good God's
providence for those who put their trust in him.
Do you want a truly striking proof? It is
before you : look at your pastor and think it
over before the good God. Oh! you say to me,
but people give to you. But who gives to me, if
not the providence of the good God? It is
there my treasures are, and nowhere else.
Alas! how blind is man to labour so hard to
damn himself, and be very unhappy even in
this world. If you only thought much of your
salvation, and of going to Mass as often as you
could, you would soon see the proof of what I
tell you." [1]

II. IN GOING TO HOLY MASS IN THE WEEK DO NOT FEAR BEING LAUGHED AT

"Do not be afraid of people saying that
that is only for those who have nothing to
do and live on their income.

"You are ashamed to serve the good God,
my friend, for fear of being despised? But

[1] Sermons, ii, 153-156.

look at him who died on the Cross : ask him
if he was ashamed to die the most humiliating death?"   Oh! accursed human respect
by which we lose "all the graces the good
God has merited for us by his death and
passion!"   But what kind of people are
those who mock?   "Poor wretches, senseless, blind. Go fearlessly on your way. They
do themselves much harm without doing you
any : pity them and go on as usual." [1]

III

"If there were only one church in the
world where the august mystery of our
altars was celebrated, and where the host
was consecrated, we should doubtless feel a
holy envy for those who stood at the doors
of that church. But we are the chosen people;
we are at the door of that place, so pure and
holy, where God is immolated every day."
Do we profit by it? "Alas! you will go three
or four leagues to earn five or six francs, and
you will not go thirty steps to hear a Mass on
week-days. Where is your faith? We have the
graces and favours of predilection, and we do
not use them : take care lest God withdraw
his gifts and entrust them to others who will
appreciate them better." [2]

"When you think of going to Mass on
working days, it is an impulse of the grace

[1] Sermons, i, 51, 54, 59, 61.
[2] *Ibid.*, i, 167, 238.

that God wills to grant you. Follow it. The saints were only sanctified by their great care to follow the good inspirations the good God sent them, and the damned have only fallen into hell because they despised them." You will be judged by the thoughts you have not welcomed, and the Masses you might have heard and have not. "Ah! great God, what will become of us then?" The flames of purgatory will be the chastisement of our laziness or of our too selfish views.[1]

EXAMPLE

M. Vianney, not seeing his parishioners growing in the love of God as he desired, and fearing his ignorance and sins to be the cause of their indifference, often called his neighbouring fellow priests to his aid. One year when he invited one of them to preach the jubilee, he had prepared souls for these devout exercises by his prayers, and especially by the celebration of the holy sacrifice. Then was seen the power of daily Mass to obtain graces of conversion and holiness. He offered it for eight days for the conversion of his parishioners, and urged all devout people to join him. The hearts of the people were so stirred, says an eyewitness, that nearly everyone began to strive with might and main to forsake sin. One would have been ashamed not to practise religion at all. The

[1] Sermons, ii, 22, 349; iv, 190.

preacher was astonished at these manifesta-
tions of faith; and at the end of the exercises,
in a sermon wherein he poured out the joy of
his heart, M.le Curé could say : "My brethren, Ars is no longer Ars. It is a great many
years since such a revolution took place in
this parish. I have been at many missions
and jubilees, but nowhere else have I found
such splendid dispositions."

The blessed Jean-Marie knew so well the
benefits of daily Mass, and appreciated so
greatly the happiness of celebrating it every
day that, after his illness in 1843, being
scarcely able to stand, he had himself carried
rather than led to the church, and, unable to
remain till day without taking food, offered
the holy sacrifice for a week at three in the
morning. He offered it the first time at the
altar of the blessed Virgin, assisted by his
good old confessor. "I would willingly live
for centuries," said a witness of this first
Mass, "if I might have before my eyes all
that time the face of that holy man renewing
the sacrifice of a life which he was receiving
anew with resignation and gratitude. His
face, marked by the sufferings and sorrows
of earth, was yet illumined with the joys of
heaven, but joys pregnant with tears and
emotion and love."

How many times at the holy Mass he asked
and received light, and words of consolation
that had been asked of his charity! "My

brother has lately been taken from me by a cruel death... and I fear for his eternal salvation," a man said to him one day... "Do tell me if I may still pray for him!" "Tomorrow, after Mass, perhaps I will answer you," replied the blessed Jean-Marie. And next day, in a voice wherein tears and hope were mingled : "My friend, let us pray!" he said, "your brother has great need of prayers."

"Then he is saved, Father!"

"Yes, but let us pray much. He is suffering and he will be delivered."

O blessed Jean-Marie, pray for me that, despising the judgements of an altogether worldly wisdom, I may appreciate and realize how fitting is the practice of hearing Mass daily.

METHOD OF HEARING HOLY MASS

WITH what dispositions should we come to holy Mass? In the presence of a God made man who immolates himself, mystically yet in a very real way, for our salvation, our hearts should be filled with faith, hope, love, contrition for our sins, and an ardent desire to receive the Victim of the sacrifice in Communion. We find models of these dispositions in the publican of the Gospel, the good thief, and the Centurion; let us meditate on them.

"The best way of hearing Mass is to unite ourselves with the priest in all he says, and to follow all his actions."

Nevertheless, here is a method which you may use profitably.

I. FROM THE BEGINNING TO THE OFFERTORY

"Be like penitents pierced with the keenest sorrow for their sins, and take for your model the *publican* in the temple. The Gospel says that he stood at the bottom of the temple, with his eyes on the ground, not daring to look at the altar, striking his breast, and saying to God, *Lord, be merciful to me a sinner.*

"*He stood at the bottom of the temple*, in the least conspicuous place, thinking himself unworthy to enter" further. "He was very different, then, from those nominal Christians who are never in a good enough place, who kneel only on a chair,[1] and who lean back in their seats with their legs crossed.

"*He kept his eyes on the ground*, so ashamed was he at the sight of his sins. He did not behave like those Christians who enter our churches with a proud, arrogant air and a kind of contempt for God's presence, and who seem to approach him like people who have nothing on their conscience that can humble them before their Creator." And yet what good reason they have to be confounded and to cast down their eyes!

He had *sincere contrition for his sins*; he knew himself guilty, and would have wished that his heart might break, for he struck his breast, says St Augustine, "to show God his regret for having offended him." He was not at all "like those people who only come to church to insult a humiliated God by their vain display of vanity and for the purpose of attracting the eyes of the world."

Oh! if we heard holy Mass in these dispositions of humility and contrition, "what graces, what blessings we should obtain! We should go away as full of heavenly blessings as the bees when they have found

[1] In many continental churches the chairs have low seats and high backs, and it is customary to turn them round during the prayers and kneel on them, leaning on the backs. — *Translator*.

more flowers than they want; we should
soon obtain pardon for our faults and grace
to persevere."

II. FROM THE OFFERTORY TO THE CONSECRATION

"Be like ministers who offer Jesus Christ
to God his Father and make him the sacrifice of all they are," and take as a good model
the *good thief* on the cross.

"What progress he makes during the
three hours that he finds himself in the company of his dying Saviour! First, he opens
the eyes of his soul to recognize his deliverer;
then, fastened to the cross, and having nothing
that remains free but his heart and tongue, he
offers both to Jesus Christ. He consecrates his
heart to him by faith and hope, and humbly
asks of him a place in Paradise; and he consecrates his tongue to him by proclaiming his
innocence and holiness : 'It is just that we
should suffer,' he says to his companion,
'but as for him, he is innocent.' He makes
himself Christ's panegyrist at a time when
others think only of outraging him, and so
great is his charity that he does all he can to
convert the other."

Like the good thief, offer Jesus your heart
to love him; consecrate your tongue to him
by using it henceforth only to glorify him and
to sing his praises; immolate yourself with
him by renouncing all that displeases him,

and by receiving the crosses he deigns to send you as a just expiation. Like the good thief, conceive a firm hope of your salvation at sight of a God who dies to secure you a place in his kingdom, and accept death in union with the divine Victim as an acknowledgement of his sovereign dominion over you.

III. FROM THE CONSECRATION TO THE END

"Consider yourselves as those who are to participate in Christ's adorable Body and precious Blood, and be inspired with the sentiments of the *Centurion* in order to communicate spiritually or sacramentally.

"The Centurion's example is so admirable, that the Church seems to take pleasure in putting it before our eyes each day at holy Mass. *Lord, I am not worthy that thou shouldst enter under my roof,* said that humble officer, *but speak only the word and my servant shall be healed...* Oh! if the good God saw in us this same humility and realisation of our nothingness, with what gladness, with what abundance of graces would he come into our hearts; what strength and courage would he give us to overcome the enemy of our salvation!" [1]

EXAMPLE

M. Vianney was neither too slow nor too quick at the altar; he studied the profit of

[1] Sermons, ii, 145-147.

all rather than his own inclination and piety.

"When I am at the altar," he used to say, "I go fairly quickly till the consecration; but when I hold our Lord in my hands I cannot go on. The thought comes to me that if I should have the unhappiness to be reprobate and separated from Jesus Christ for eternity, I should at least have had the happiness of holding him in my hands as long as possible." [1] Then a smile like an angel's would be seen on his lips, and his face would appear shining with ecstasy.

"When serving his Mass," said a pilgrim, "I had the opportunity of noticing the only part over which he was longer than other priests, and this was before the Communion." The liturgical prayers being ended, there was mysterious converse, outwardly visible, between our Lord Jesus Christ and his servant. M. Vianney gazed lovingly at the sacred Host. His lips uttered words : he stopped, listened, replied, and then with a visible effort of friend parting from friend, he consumed the sacred species.

Those at Mass would marvel at the devotion, modesty, and gravity with which he celebrated the holy mysteries. Many people placed themselves where they could see him at the elevation, and there were some among them who dared not continue to look upon

[1] *Sommaire.*

that sight : he was like an angel, they said,
and seemed to be in heaven.

A stranger, having made his confession to
M. le Curé, and being unwilling to make up
his mind to do what was demanded of him,
had gone abruptly out of the church in much
displeasure.   He decided, nevertheless, to
come to Mass before leaving next day.   He
was so much struck by the expression of
M. Vianney's face at the moment of the Communion that he was converted.

O blessed Jean-Marie, pray for us and procure us the grace to assist at the holy sacrifice of the Mass with the faith, humility,
contrition, and love with which you yourself
were filled in celebrating it.

AFTER HOLY MASS

THE Gospel says that after celebrating the first Mass in the Cenacle, our Lord sang a hymn with his Apostles.[1] Whence St John Chrysostom concludes that the believer who is present at the holy sacrifice ought not to withdraw till he has thanked God for this priceless grace. His heart ought to be divided between gratitude, wonder, and a firm resolution to sin no more.

I. GRATITUDE

"Before leaving the church after holy Mass never fail to thank God for the graces he has just given you."

You have a form of thanksgiving in your prayer-books : read it. At least, praise God, bless him for having allowed you to take part in the most august mystery of religion; and pray the blessed Virgin to praise and bless him with you.

II. WONDER

"Go home completely occupied by what you have seen.

"It is said in the Holy Scriptures that the Queen of Saba, having heard such glorious

[1] St Matt. 26. 30.

things spoken of Solomon and the marvels that were performed in his country, desired to see them for herself. But when she had seen the glories of the temple and the fair harmony which reigned there, she went back declaring that all she had been told was nothing in comparison with what her eyes had seen. Those marvels remained deeply graven on her heart.

"That is exactly what would happen to us on leaving our churches if we paid careful attention to all that happens during our holy and awful mysteries. In Solomon's temple it was" a man's work that was seen; "here it is God himself who acts and works infinite miracles. Solomon's temple was destined to hold a little manna and the Tables of the Law; but in our churches, ah! great God! it is Jesus Christ himself who sheds his Blood and immolates himself daily on our altars to his Father's justice for our sins. These are marvels so great that the more we examine them the more incomprehensible we find them.

III. A FIRM RESOLUTION TO SIN NO MORE

"A Christian, at the close of the sacred services, moved by thoughts which the prayers and the sight of the ceremonies have aroused in him, ought to say to himself : 'I have just assisted at holy Mass; a God has immolated himself for me and shed his blood for the salvation of our souls : what could he do more? Oh! wretch that I am, who for so many years have refused him my heart which he created only for himself and which he asks of me that he may make it happy! I have just sung the praises of God with this same mouth that I have so many times defiled with all kinds of sins.' " O my God, shall my tongue always be used now to praise thee and now to slight thee? No, Lord, henceforth I want only to bless and love thee.

"No Christian who goes away without these thoughts in his heard has assisted at the sacred services with the dispositions that he ought to have." [1]

EXAMPLE

As a young man M. Vianney had himself observed the touching recommendations which, as curé, he addressed to his parishioners, and he was only recalling, without thinking of it, a practice dear to his boyhood. At Dardilly, in fact, Jean-Marie went to the church on Sundays long before the faithful were assembled there, and he did not leave it till long after them. He used to say that preparation and thanksgiving before and after the holy sacrifice are necessary to a Christian if he does not wish to be ungrateful, or to treat lightly the gifts which Jesus Christ makes to him in immolating himself on the altar.

[1] *Sermons*, iv, 230-233.

At Nöes also everyone was edified by his devotion before the Blessed Sacrament, and, as at Dardilly, it was very soon noticed that he remained in the church after holy Mass when all the others had gone.

He was seen to be always modest, recollected, exemplary in his conduct, and zealous in the fulfilment of his duties : everyone was charmed with him, and people used to come from neighbouring parishes to pray and sing hymns with him.

O blessed Jean-Marie, pray for us and obtain us grace never to receive God's gifts without grateful hearts.

AFTERWORD

This edition of a book first published in English in 1923, two years prior to the canonization of St. John Vianney, will bring some of the humble Saint's work into the twenty-first century. Demand in North America and Britain occasions the re-publication, and it is germane to consider why there should be such interest now in the once private meditations of an ill-educated clergyman of a very obscure French village.

St. John did not leave a great body of spiritual writing. His sermons, though meticulously prepared, were usually short and without ornamentation. It has been said that he prayed rather than preached the homily. And yet the care with which his sayings have been preserved speaks of their importance.

He was not the most likely candidate for the priesthood, a peasant growing up during the post-revolutionary Reign of Terror during which priests and religious were invariably suppressed, and many guillotined. His first seminary was an ad-hoc affair in the rectory of Father Balley.

He failed repeatedly in his classes to the point that his colleagues found his answers embarrassing. It was only the fact of the dearth of priests that made John Vianney a candidate at all, and were it not for the inspiration of Fr. Balley and his Vicar-General (who remarked that the Church needed above all *holy* priests) even that emergency might not have made for his ordination. And yet, St. John is now revered as the patron of all parish priests.

It is not difficult to understand how the extraordinary piety of the Curé d'Ars, over the course of forty years, won his village and much of the world beyond, for Christ. However it is remarkable that the same prayerful humility should translate without hermeneutic to our own quite different time and setting.

Then perhaps, our complex and abrasive urban society is not too far removed from post-Napoleonic Ars. Where Ars was a spiritual and economic shambles, the farming families reduced by repeated conscription, the once-productive fields untilled and unwatered, the mill in ruins, the wells fetid, the church empty, —there are obvious parallels in our world. The relentless dissolution of our current social and economic systems, the facts, for instance, that a fifth of American children are born into poverty, and that our unintegrated technologies produce air and water so toxic that no earthly power can mitigate their effects, —end the idea that humanity can prosper without constant prayer, humbly, eucharistically opening itself to God's grace.

After the Curé had trudged the unmade roads to his new parish, and found in the fog, the dispiriting church building, he simply knelt on the cold flagstones and prayed. We cannot say what or how he prayed, but as the first act he undertook on entering the village, it commends itself. If we are to look to Saints for our examples, then this must be a most important one: to preface any undertaking with prayer.

Lesser people might have been inclined instantly to set about redressing injustices, collecting money, preaching fine sermons, mortaring bricks together. But for the Saint, prayer was sufficient, all else would follow. That same morning, when the curious parishioners had attended mass, several remarked on the holiness of the new Curé. Unexpectedly, in the following days their number swelled, confessions were heard, the sick were blessed, some were encouraged enough to depart from custom and to come before the altar to receive the Savior in Holy Communion.

Participation in the mystery of the Eucharist was for the villagers of Ars, as for we who succeed them, the means whereby they were lifted above their drudging, sinful despair.

But in Ars, the New Life was so marked that it was clear something miraculous was taking place. It is reported that families were strengthened from within, the young adults were no longer inclined to leave the village. More fields were tilled, the cattle more carefully tended, drinking establishments closed for lack of custom, feuding neighbors were reconciled, spare moments were spent before the Blessed Sacrament in the little church, itself no longer a neglected hull, but the focal point of a true community.

Ars would never become wealthy in earthly terms, the wars and usurious taxes prevented that, but it had now undergone its conversion. The lesson for our own time is easily learned, if only there is a will, and the faith to learn it.

"It is faith we want. Ask God to open the eyes of your heart. If you say to our Lord sincerely, like the blind man in Jericho: 'O Lord, make me to see!' you will certainly obtain what you desire."

—CATECHISM ON THE REAL PRESENCE.